READING ABOUT SCIENCE
Skills and Concepts

John F. Mongillo
Ray Broekel
Beth S. Atwood
Donald L. Buchholz
Albert B. Carr
Claudia Cornett
Jacqueline L. Harris
Vivian Zwaik

Special Reading Consultant
Roger Farr
    Professor of Education
    Indiana University

WEBSTER DIVISION
McGRAW-HILL BOOK COMPANY

New York   St. Louis   San Francisco   Auckland   Bogotá
Düsseldorf   Johannesburg   London   Madrid   Mexico
Montreal   New Delhi   Panama   Paris   São Paulo   Singapore
Sydney   Tokyo   Toronto

A

Sponsoring Editor: Joanne E. Kane
Managing Editor: Alma Graham
Coordinating Editor: Mary Ann Jones
Production Manager: Karen Romano
Design Supervisor: Margaret Amirassefi
Photo Editing Supervisor: Rosemary O'Connell
Photo Editor: Suzanne Volkman

Photo Research: Randy Matusow
Design and Production: Two Twenty Two Design
Illustrator: Sylvia Stone

This book was set in twelve-point Century Schoolbook by Monotype Composition Company, Inc.

PHOTO CREDITS

12—George Porter/Photo Researchers; **14**—Jen and Des Bartlett/Photo Researchers; **16**—San Diego Zoological Society; **18,20**—Tom McHugh/Photo Researchers; **22**—Hugh Spencer/Photo Researchers; **24**—Wide World Photos; **26**—Jen and Des Bartlett/Photo Researchers; **28**—Jack Donnelly/Woods Hole Oceanographic Institution, Dr. Kathleen Crane/Woods Hole Oceanographic Institution; **30**—National Diary Council; **32**—Christa Armstrong/Photo Researchers; **34**—National Zoological Park; **36**—Anita Sabarese; **38**—Burpee Seeds; **40**—Anita Sabarese; **42**—Randy Matusow/McGraw-Hill; **43**—Cleveland Health Museum; **48**—NASA; **52**—Alan Pitcairn/Grant Heilman; **54,56**—NASA; **58**—United States Air Force; **60**—United States Navy; **62**—American Association for the Advancement of Science; **64**—John Porteous/Woods Hole Oceanographic Institution; **66**—ABC/TV; **67**—Alabama Space & Rocket Center; **72**—Mimi Forsyth/Monkmeyer; **74**—Joan Lifton/Woodfin Camp & Associates; **76**—Betty Adams/Monkmeyer; **78**—Culver Pictures; **80**—U.S. Environmental Protection Agency; **82**—Robert Capece/McGraw-Hill; **84**—Harvey Stein; **86**—Billings Energy Corporation; **88**—Robert Capece/McGraw-Hill; **90**—Jodi Ellers; **91**—Museum of Science and Industry; **97**—American Museum of Natural History, Grant Heilman; **98**—American Museum of Natural History, R.W. Fairbridge/Columbia University.

Cover photograph by Jim Adair/The Image Bank.

ISBN 0-07-002421-9

Copyright © 1981 by McGraw-Hill, Inc. All Rights Reserved. Printed in the United States of America. No part of this publication may be reproduced, stored in a retrieval system, or transmitted, in any form or by any means, electronic, mechanical, photocopying, recording, or otherwise, without the prior written permission of the publisher.

AUTHORS

John F. Mongillo
Editor in Chief, Science Department
Webster Division
McGraw-Hill Book Company
New York, New York

Dr. Ray Broekel
Author and Consultant
Ipswich, Massachusetts

Beth S. Atwood
Writer and Reading Consultant
Durham, Connecticut

Donald L. Buchholz
Developer of Curriculum Materials
Honolulu, Hawaii

Albert B. Carr
Professor of Science Education
University of Hawaii
Honolulu, Hawaii

Claudia Cornett
Assistant Professor of Education
Wittenberg University
Springfield, Ohio

Jacqueline L. Harris
Writer and Science Editor
Wethersfield, Connecticut

Vivian Zwaik
Writer and Educational Consultant
Glen Head, New York

Contributing Writers

Rita Harkins Dickinson
Special Education Instructor
Rio Salado Community College
Phoenix, Arizona

Myra J. Goldberg
Reading Consultant
Rye, New York

Adrienne Ballard Taylor
Junior High School Science Teacher
Black Mountain School
Cave Creek, Arizona

Bruce Tone
Editorial Associate
School of Education
Indiana University
Bloomington, Indiana

Dr. Clifford Watson
Staff Coordinator
Region 1
Detroit Public Schools
Detroit, Michigan

Reviewers

Del Alberti
Principal, John Muir School
Merced, California

Josephine D. Duckett
Elementary Science Resource Teacher
Charlotte-Mecklenburg School System
Charlotte, North Carolina

Dr. Alice Kimber Hankla
Physics Consultant
Atlanta, Georgia

Lola Hanson Harris
Curriculum Specialist
Figueroa Street Elementary School
Los Angeles, California

Jerry Hayes
Science Coordinator
Bureau of Science
Chicago, Illinois

Kent A. Hinshaw
Supervisor of Science
St. Paul Public Schools
St. Paul, Minnesota

Lois Kaylor
Reading Resource Teacher
New Castle Junior High School
New Castle, Delaware

Penny Miller
Reading Specialist
C.E.S.A. 6
Chippewa Falls, Wisconsin

Mary Nalbandian
Director of Science
Chicago Board of Education
Chicago, Illinois

Dr. Martha Piper
Associate Professor of Education
College of Education
University of Houston
Houston, Texas

Dr. Ronald D. Simpson
Professor of Science Education
North Carolina State University
Raleigh, North Carolina

Arlene B. Soifer
Administrator for Educational Programs
Nassau B.O.C.E.S.
Westbury, New York

Patricia Towle
Title I Reading Teacher
McCarthy Elementary School
Framingham, Massachusetts

PRONUNCIATION GUIDE

Some words in this book may be unfamiliar to you and difficult for you to pronounce. These words are printed in italics. Then, they are spelled according to the way they are said, or pronounced. This phonetic spelling appears in parentheses next to the words. The pronunciation guide below will help you say the words.

ă	pat	î	dear, deer, fierce, mere	p	pop	zh	garage, pleasure; vision
ā	aid, fey, pay			r	roar		
â	air, care, wear	j	judge	s	miss, sauce, see	ə	about, silent pencil, lemon, circus
ä	father	k	cat, kick, pique	sh	dish, ship		
b	bib	l	lid, needle	t	tight		
ch	church	m	am, man, mum	th	path, thin	ər	butter
d	deed	n	no, sudden	th	bathe, this		
ĕ	pet, pleasure	ng	thing	ŭ	cut, rough		
ē	be, bee, easy, leisure	ŏ	horrible, pot	û	circle, firm, heard, term, turn, urge, word		
		ō	go, hoarse, row, toe				STRESS
f	fast, fife, off, phase, rough	ô	alter, caught, for, paw	v	cave, valve, vine		Primary stress ′ **bi·ol′o·gy** [bī ŏl′ejē]
g	gag			w	with		
h	hat	oi	boy, noise, oil	y	yes		Secondary stress ′ **bi′o·log′i·cal** [bī′elŏj′ĭkel]
hw	which	ou	cow, out	yōō	abuse, use		
ĭ	pit	ŏŏ	took	z	rose, size, xylophone, zebra		
ī	by, guy, pie	ōō	boot, fruit				

The key to pronunciation above is reprinted by permission from *The American Heritage School Dictionary* copyright © 1977, by Houghton Mifflin Company.

TABLE OF CONTENTS

	Page
To the Student	8
Life Science	12
A Living Dragon	14
When the Bears Turned Green	16
Where Have All the Eagles Gone?	18
The Lungfish	20
Hide and Seek	22
Finger Talk	24
Ants That Look for Leaves	26
A Strange World Under the Sea	28
Think Before You Eat	30
Your Teeth and You	32
Black and White All Over	34
Meet the Cactus	36
Sugar Snap Peas	38
The Ginkgo Tree	40
People To Know	
Dr. Jane Wright	42
Places To Go	
A Visit to the Cleveland Health Education Museum	43

	Page
Puzzles To Do	
Animals of North America	44
Insects	45
Science Adventures	
A Food Record	46
Earth-Space Science	48
A Deadly Dinosaur	50
A Black Graveyard for Animals	52
Moon Rocks Tell Many Secrets	54
Is There Life on Mars?	56
Hurricane Watch	58
Cool, Clear Water	60
Mountains of Ice	62
All Aboard the Alvin	64
People To Know	
Jacques Cousteau	66
Places To Go	
A Visit to the Alabama Space and Rocket Center	67

	Page		Page

Puzzles To Do
The Earth — 68
Weather — 69

Science Adventures
A Weather Record — 70

Physical Science
Hang Gliding — 74
Hot-Air Balloon — 76
Sailboats Go Back to Work — 78
What Do You Think? — 80
How a Battery Works — 82
Solar Heat — 84
Fuel for Tomorrow — 86
The Uses of Petroleum — 88

People To Know
Wind Power for School Lights — 90

Places To Go
A Visit to the Museum of Science and Industry — 91

Puzzles To Do
An Energy Source — 92
Products from Oil — 93

Science Adventures
Investigating Paper Airplanes — 94

Careers in Science — 96

Words to Know — 102
Keeping a Record of Your Progress — 105
Bibliography — 107
Metric Tables — 110

TO THE STUDENT

The world of science is a world of observing, exploring, predicting, reading, experimenting, testing, and recording. It is a world of trying and failing and trying again until, at last, you succeed. In the world of science, there is always some exciting discovery to be made and something new to explore.

In this book, you will learn about some of these explorations and discoveries. Through these readings about science, you will have a chance to join the crew of the *Alvin* and explore the strange world beneath the sea. You may hop aboard a hot-air balloon and float across the Atlantic Ocean or track cougars through the Rocky Mountains. You will learn that science is an important part of your life—and that reading about science is fun.

Three Areas of Science

READING ABOUT SCIENCE explores three areas of science: life science, earth-space science, and physical science. Each book in this series contains a unit on each of the three areas. Although there are different areas of science, it is important to remember that each area is related to the others in some way and that all areas are important to people.

Life science is the study of living things. Life scientists explore the world of plants, animals, and humans. Their goal is to find out how living things depend upon each other for survival and to observe how they live and interact in their environments, or surroundings.

The general area of life science includes many specialized areas, such as botany, zoology, and ecology. *Botanists* work mainly with plants. *Zoologists* work mostly with animals. *Ecologists* are scientists who study the effects of air pollution, water pollution, and noise pollution on living things.

Earth-space science is the study of our Earth and other bodies in the solar system. Some earth-space scientists are *meteorologists,* who study climate and weather; *geologists,* who study the earth, the way it was formed and its makeup, rocks and fossils, earthquakes, and volcanoes; *oceanographers,* who study currents, waves, and life in the oceans of the world; and *astronomers,* who study the solar system, including the sun and other stars, moons, and planets.

Physical science is the study of matter and energy. *Physicists* are physical scientists who explore topics such as matter, atoms, and nuclear energy. Other physical scientists study sound, magnetism, heat, light, electricity, water, and air. *Chemists* develop the substances used in medicine, clothing, food, and many other things.

All of these areas of science influence our everyday life. For example, our transportation and communications systems depend on the work of physical scientists. Together, physical scientists, earth-space scientists, and life scientists search for ways to solve problems and improve the quality of our everyday life.

In your reading, you may discover that there is one area of science that you like especially. The bibliography in the back of this book is divided into life, earth-space, and physical sciences. The books that are suggested will take you on more adventures in the world of science.

Reading Science Materials

Some students are nervous about taking courses in science. They think that science is too difficult, and so they give up even before they begin.

Think about this. Do you enjoy the world around you? Do you ever wonder why clouds have so many different shapes and what keeps planes up in the air? Did you ever want to explore a cave or find out why volcanoes erupt or why the earth shakes? If you can answer yes to any of those questions and if you are willing to read and think and investigate carefully the world around you, then you can do well in science and enjoy it, too!

Reading science materials is different from reading a magazine or a novel. You must take your time and think about what you are reading. Remember that science materials contain special vocabulary words. You will know some words. Other words may be familiar to you, but you may be unsure of their meanings. And still other words may be totally unfamiliar. It is these unfamiliar words in particular that make science reading seem difficult.

Steps to Follow

The suggestions that follow will help you use this book:

A. Study the photo or drawing that goes with the story. Read the title and the sentences that are printed in blue. These are all clues to what the story is about.

B. Study the words for the story in the list of Words to Know in the back of this book. You will find it easier to read the story if you understand the meanings of these words. Many times, you will find the meaning of the word right in the story.

When reading the story, look for clues to important words or ideas. Vocabulary words appear in a special print. Sometimes words or phrases are underlined. Pay special attention to these clues.

C. Read the story carefully. Think about what you are reading. Are any of the ideas in the story things that you have heard or read about before?

D. As you read, ask yourself questions. For example, "Why did the electricity go off?" "What caused the bears to turn green?" Many times, your questions are answered later in the story. Questioning helps you to understand what the author is saying. Asking questions also gets you ready for what comes next in the story.

E. Pay special attention to diagrams, charts, and other visual aids. They will often help you to understand the story better.

F. After you read the story slowly and carefully, you are ready to answer the questions on the Questions page. If the book you have is part of a classroom set, you should write your answers in a special notebook or on paper that you can keep in a folder. Do not write in this book without your teacher's permission.

Put your name, the title of the story, and its page number on a sheet of paper. Read each question carefully. Record the question number and your answer on your answer paper.

The questions in this book check for the following kinds of comprehension, or understanding:

1. *Science vocabulary comprehension*. This kind of question asks you to remember the meaning of a word or term used in the story.

2. *Literal comprehension*. This kind of question asks you to remember certain facts that are given in the story. For example, the story might state that a snake was over 5 meters long. A literal question would ask you: "How long was the snake?"

3. *Interpretive comprehension*. This kind of question asks you to think about the story. To answer the question, you must decide what the author means, not what is said, or stated, in the story. For example, you may be

asked what the *main idea* of the story is or what happened first, or what *caused* something to happen in the story.

4. *Applied comprehension.* This kind of question asks you to use what you have read to (1) solve a new problem, (2) interpret a chart or graph; or (3) put a certain topic under its correct heading, or category.

You should read each question carefully. You may go back to the story to help you find the answer. The questions are meant to help you learn how to read science better.

G. When you complete the Questions page, turn it in to your teacher. Or, with your teacher's permission, check your answers against the answer key in the *Teacher's Guide.* If you made a mistake, find out what you did wrong. Practice answering that kind of question, and you will do better the next time.

H. Turn to the directions that tell you how to keep your Progress Charts. If you are not supposed to write in this book, you may make a copy of each chart to keep in your READING ABOUT SCIENCE folder or notebook. You may be surprised to see how well you can read science.

Special Sections

There are some special sections that follow each of the three science units.

People to Know is about a person or a group of people who have done something special in the field of life science, earth-space science, or physical science. Some examples are Margaret Seddon, astronaut; Jacques Cousteau, undersea explorer; Benjamin Banneker, astronomer; and Mary Jean Currier, wildlife scientist.

Places to Go takes you on visits to aquariums, zoos, space centers, and museums all over the United States and in Canada.

Puzzles to Do includes crossword puzzles, hidden-word games, and mazes on many different topics in science.

Science Adventures gives you a chance to investigate interesting topics such as solar energy, making fossils, and extrasensory perception.

The last unit in the book is a special unit called Careers in Science. This unit gives you an opportunity to investigate hundreds of science-related careers.

You may decide to make science your lifelong hobby or even your career. Whatever you do, the authors of READING ABOUT SCIENCE hope that this book will help you discover the joys of science.

LIFE SCIENCE

You have probably seen many frogs. But have you ever seen a giant tree frog? These amphibians *are found in warm, humid climates. They grow to be about 13 centimeters long. (Some tree frogs are only 2 centimeters long.) When the male frog sings, it makes a snarling, snorting sound. Imagine the noise when hundreds of tree frogs are singing!*

A Living Dragon

Are there really living dragons?

It is morning on the island of *Komodo* (kə mō′dō) in the Indian Ocean. Out of a cave comes a giant animal. It sticks out a long forked tongue. Inside its red mouth are rows of teeth. Is this a dream? No! There is such an animal. It is called the Komodo dragon.

The Komodo dragon is a *monitor lizard* (mŏn′ĭ tər lĭz′ərd), the largest of all known lizards. It can grow as long as 330 centimeters and weigh as much as 2 people. The Komodo looks for food by smelling with its tongue. This giant lizard can eat pigs, deer, goats, and monkeys.

For hundreds of years, people have talked about dragons as make-believe. Then, in 1912, people heard about the Komodo dragon. They thought it, too, was make-believe. But first four Komodo skins and then photographs were brought back from the island. Now, people knew that the Komodo dragon was *real*.

QUESTIONS

1. The *monitor lizard* is
    a. a small lizard with many rows of teeth.
    b. a make-believe lizard.
    c. the largest known lizard in the world.

2. The Komodo dragon uses its tongue to
    a. catch snakes.
    b. scare people.
    c. smell food.

3. People may not have believed the Komodo dragon was real because
    a. they had never seen one themselves.
    b. the dragon was not alive until 1912.
    c. the dragon never came out of its cave.

4. Which of the following happened *first?*
    a. People saw photographs of the Komodo.
    b. Komodo skins were brought back from the island.
    c. People knew that the Komodo was real.

5. According to the story, which of the following statements is *true?*
    a. All the stories about the Komodo dragon were make-believe.
    b. Sometimes what we think is make-believe turns out to be real.
    c. People who saw the Komodo dragon were dreaming.

When the Bears Turned Green

Read all about the zoo bears that turned green.

Polar bears are supposed to be white. They live in the cold northern parts of the world. Their white fur makes them almost invisible in the snow and ice.

But three bears living in a zoo turned green. That's right! The big white bears turned as green as grass. Scientists wondered why it had happened. They cut away some of the bears' fur and looked at it carefully. There were tiny plants called *algae* (ăl′jē) inside the bears' fur. Algae are plants that grow mostly in water, and they do not have true leaves or flowers.

Some kinds of algae can be green, and it was this algae that changed the color of the bears' fur. Scientists believe the algae were living in the small pool used by the bears. When the bears went for a swim, the algae moved into the bears' fur. The algae are not hurting the bears. The bears are not hurting the algae. In fact, they live together happily. But green polar bears are a strange sight!

QUESTIONS

1. *Algae* are
    a. a kind of bear.
    b. tiny plants.
    c. plants with flowers.

2. Algae live
    a. in the water.
    b. in dry places.
    c. only in zoos.

3. The bears turned green because
    a. they were sick.
    b. they went swimming too often.
    c. there were plants in their fur.

4. Polar bears can live safely in ice and snow because
    a. their white color makes it hard for hunters to see them.
    b. they can see hunters coming from far away.
    c. people do not hunt where there is ice and snow.

5. In this story, where were the algae before they got into the bears' fur?
    a. in the snow
    b. in the flowers
    c. in the pool

Where Have All the Eagles Gone?

What is happening to the bald eagle?

The bald eagle is a big, beautiful bird. It has a snow-white head. The eagle's wingspread is more than 2 meters.

The bald eagle once lived near lakes and rivers in many parts of North America. But one year, bird watchers found that fewer and fewer eagle eggs were hatching. The bald eagle had become an endangered animal. It was in danger of disappearing.

Why were these birds endangered? One reason is that people were cutting down many trees where eagles nested, or lived. Also, people were using the chemical DDT to kill insects. The DDT was carried by the wind to lakes and rivers. When the mother eagle ate the fish from these waters, she also ate the DDT. This made the shells of her eggs so thin that they broke under her in the nest. Because of this, the eggs did not hatch.

Today, there is a law against using DDT. There are also laws that set aside places where animals can safely build their homes.

QUESTIONS

1. When fewer and fewer eagle eggs hatched each year, bird watchers knew that the bald eagle had become _____ animal.
    a. an endangered
    b. a dangerous
    c. a plentiful

2. The eagles left their nests when
    a. the baby eagles were hatched.
    b. people passed laws against eagles' living in trees.
    c. people began to cut down trees where eagles lived.

3. Fewer eagle eggs were hatching because
    a. mother eagles were not laying as many eggs.
    b. DDT was killing the baby eagles.
    c. DDT made the shell of the eagle egg very thin.

4. The law against using DDT is a good law because
    a. DDT kills bugs and insects that are harmful.
    b. DDT endangers birds, fish, and other animals.
    c. DDT made the eagles bald.

5. The bald eagle got its name because
    a. from a distance, the snow-white feathers make its head look bald.
    b. the DDT made the feathers on its head fall off.
    c. eagles do not have feathers on their heads.

The Lungfish

Did you ever hear of a fish that can live for a long time without being in water?

The lungfish breathes through gills just as other fish do. But unlike other fish, it also has lungs. So the lungfish can breathe air just as animals living on land do. For this reason, a lungfish can live for a long time without being in the water.

Most lungfish live in Africa, where they are found in shallow lakes and rivers. Sometimes, very little rain falls. Then, the shallow lakes and rivers dry up, and the other fish in the river die. What happens to a lungfish? It curls up into a ball in the mud at the bottom of the lake or river. Then, it begins to breathe with its lungs instead of its gills.

If necessary, a lungfish can live this way for as long as three or four years. When the rains come, the lungfish straightens itself out. And it begins swimming around in the water again—almost as if nothing had happened!

QUESTIONS

1. A lungfish is *different* from other fish because it
    - a. can breathe through either lungs or gills.
    - b. has gills to breathe through but no lungs.
    - c. is not able to breathe air.

2. Most lungfish are found
    - a. in the deep waters of the ocean.
    - b. in shallow lakes or rivers.
    - c. on the shores of rivers.

3. A lungfish can live out of water for
    - a. three or four years.
    - b. more than six years.
    - c. less than four hours.

4. In the story, what happens *first?*
    - a. The lungfish curls up into a ball.
    - b. The river dries up.
    - c. The lungfish breathes through its lungs.

5. You could say that the lungfish is lucky because
    - a. it can live either in water or on land.
    - b. it need never live in water.
    - c. it lives where there is plenty of rain.

Hide and Seek

Their color and markings help animals to hide.

Look at the picture of the moth. The moth is not easy to see because it is almost the same color as the bark on the tree. The moth's coloring is a kind of *camouflage* (kăm′ə fläzh′). This coloring, or camouflage, helps the moth hide from its enemies.

Many animals have colors and markings that make them hard to see. A white polar bear is hard to see against the snow. In the water, an alligator looks like a floating log. Cheetahs have spots, and zebras have stripes. These markings camouflage the animals' bodies so their enemies cannot see them.

Color also hides insects. Some insects look like sticks and stems. Grasshoppers are as green as the plants they eat. In one forest, an insect is bright pink. It hides on pink flowers.

Look at the animals where you live. List the animals that are hard to see. How many did you find?

QUESTIONS

1. *Camouflage* is important to many animals because
    a. it helps the animals hide from their enemies.
    b. other animals can find them more easily.
    c. it makes them look green.

2. In the water, an alligator
    a. turns green in color.
    b. looks like a floating log.
    c. cannot hide easily.

3. Spots or stripes on animals are also known as
    a. colors.
    b. bark.
    c. markings.

4. If a moth were on a green leaf,
    a. you could not see it easily.
    b. it would be easy to see.
    c. its enemies could not find it.

5. The *main idea* of this story is that
    a. many animals are protected from harm because of their color.
    b. polar bears live in the snow.
    c. some insects are bright pink and live in the forest.

Finger Talk

Can animals learn to "talk"?

Koko the gorilla wants a drink. So she asks for it. She sees a picture of the three little kittens who lost their mittens. They are being scolded by their mother, and Koko knows that they are crying. She can tell you that the kittens' mother scolds them when they do something "bad."

Koko says "drink" and "bad" by using her fingers. Penny Patterson, Koko's teacher, also talks with her fingers. If Patterson wants Koko to learn the word *ball*, she shows Koko a ball. Then she shapes Koko's fingers into the "finger-talk" word for *ball*. Finger talk is like sign language.

Koko was born on July 4, 1971. She has a vocabulary of more than 400 words, and she is the first gorilla to learn finger talk. If you ever meet a gorilla who makes fast, funny shapes with her fingers, you will know that it is Koko and that she is talking to you!

QUESTIONS

1. *Finger talk* is
    a. a kind of sign language.
    b. used only by people who speak.
    c. a new way to read.

2. Penny Patterson teaches Koko to
    a. talk with her fingers.
    b. read a book.
    c. talk just like humans.

3. Koko knows that the kittens have done something "bad" because she can
    a. talk with her fingers.
    b. read the words in the book with her fingers.
    c. understand what is happening in the picture.

4. If Penny Patterson wanted to teach Koko the word *mitten*, she would
    a. write the word *mitten* on a pad and point to it.
    b. show Koko a mitten and shape the gorilla's hands into the finger-talk word for *mitten*.
    c. show Koko a mitten and say the word *mitten* over and over again until Koko could say it.

5. "Finger Talk" might also have been called
    a. "Koko and the Three Little Kittens."
    b. "Koko, the Talking Gorilla."
    c. "A Teacher Named Penny."

Ants That Look for Leaves

Did you ever hear of the leaf-cutting ant?

What kind of ant cuts off bits of leaves? The ant is called the leaf-cutting ant, and it lives in parts of Central America and South America.

Leaf-cutting ants build their nests under the ground. Many of them go out to search for leaves. They march along one after the other. The ants stop when they find a tree or bush. Each ant cuts off a piece of leaf. Then the ants march back to their nest carrying the leaf pieces over their heads.

The ants chew up the leaf pieces, but they do not eat them. Instead, they place the wet, chewed-up leaves in the nest. Plants called *fungi* (fŭn′jī′) begin to grow on the leaves. The nest gets no sunlight and is a good growing place for some kinds of fungi. The ants then eat the fungi.

QUESTIONS

1. *Fungi* are
    a. leaves.
    b. plants.
    c. animals.

2. Leaf-cutting ants are found
    a. in parts of Central America and South America.
    b. all over the world.
    c. only in South America.

3. Where do leaf-cutting ants hold the pieces of leaves when they march?
    a. in their mouths
    b. over their heads
    c. on their heads

4. In the story, which of the following things happens *first*?
    a. The ants put bits of leaves in their nest.
    b. The ants chew up bits of leaves.
    c. The ants eat the fungi.

5. One reason fungi grow on the wet, chewed-up leaves is that
    a. the ants have put the leaves in a dark place.
    b. all fungi grow best in places where there is no light.
    c. the leaves come from a special kind of bush.

 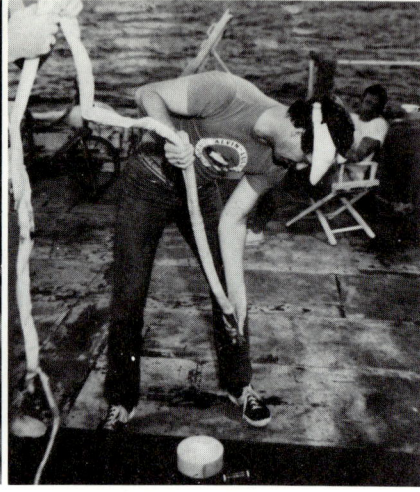

A Strange World under the Sea

Discovered: strange animals under the sea!

It is like another world. The sun never shines there. It is a place far beneath the sea. The ocean water is very hot and full of *chemicals* (kĕm′ĭ kəlz). It is a real place that has just been found.

For many years, scientists did not know about this undersea place. They had no way to travel safely to places deep under the sea. But now, scientists can make the trip in small underwater ships called *submarines* (sŭb′mə rēnz′).

The scientists have seen many strange water animals in those dark waters. "It was like going to Disneyland," said one scientist. He saw red worms as thick and as long as a jump rope. Giant sea spiders, as big as dinner plates, moved among the rocks. Animals that looked like flowers floated in the water.

How did these strange animals come to be? Why don't they live on land? So far, these are the only animals scientists know of that could live in the deep undersea world.

QUESTIONS

1. A *submarine* is
    a. an animal that lives underwater.
    b. an underwater ship.
    c. a chemical found underwater.

2. In a dark, deep place beneath the sea, scientists saw
    a. strange animals.
    b. a strange ship.
    c. lots of sunlight.

3. The worms the scientists saw
    a. were as big as dinner plates.
    b. looked like flowers.
    c. were thick and long.

4. Why has this strange part of the ocean only just been discovered?
    a. Until now, there was no safe way to get there.
    b. Scientists never wanted to go there before now.
    c. People thought that the animals living there were dangerous.

5. Under which of the headings below would you put the red worms?
    a. Underwater Plants
    b. Strange Land Animals
    c. Unusual Undersea Animals

Think before You Eat

Why should you watch what you eat?

"Drink your milk! Finish your vegetables! Have some fruit instead of eating that candy!"

Most of us have heard these words. But do we know why one food is better for us than another? It is because some foods have more *nutrients* (nōō'trē ənts) than others. And all plants and animals need nutrients to grow and to stay strong. Your body needs them, too.

You get nutrients from the foods you eat. Different foods have different nutrients, and no one food has all the nutrients your body needs. So you must eat some foods from each of the four groups in the picture above. And you must eat them every day.

As you grow, your body will change, and you will need a different number of servings from each food group each day. So think before you eat. Be sure to get as many nutrients as you can from the foods you eat.

QUESTIONS

1. People, animals, and plants all need _____ to grow and to stay strong.
    a. fruits
    b. grains
    c. nutrients

2. We get most of the nutrients we need from _____ food groups.
    a. two
    b. three
    c. four

3. When people get older, they probably _____ from each food group each day.
    a. need the same number of servings
    b. do not need any servings
    c. need a different number of servings

Use the chart below to answer questions 4 and 5.

BASIC FOUR FOOD GROUPS

Group	Foods	Daily Servings
Dairy	milk, cheese, ice cream	4 or more
Grain	bread, cereal, rice, noodles	4 or more
Fruits and Vegetables	oranges, grapes, green beans, peas	4 or more
Meat and Poultry	beef, pork, chicken, eggs, fish	2 or more

4. Which of the following belongs to the Grain Group?
    a. breads
    b. oranges
    c. eggs

5. Your body needs at least two servings of food from the _____ Group each day.
    a. Dairy
    b. Meat and Poultry
    c. Grain

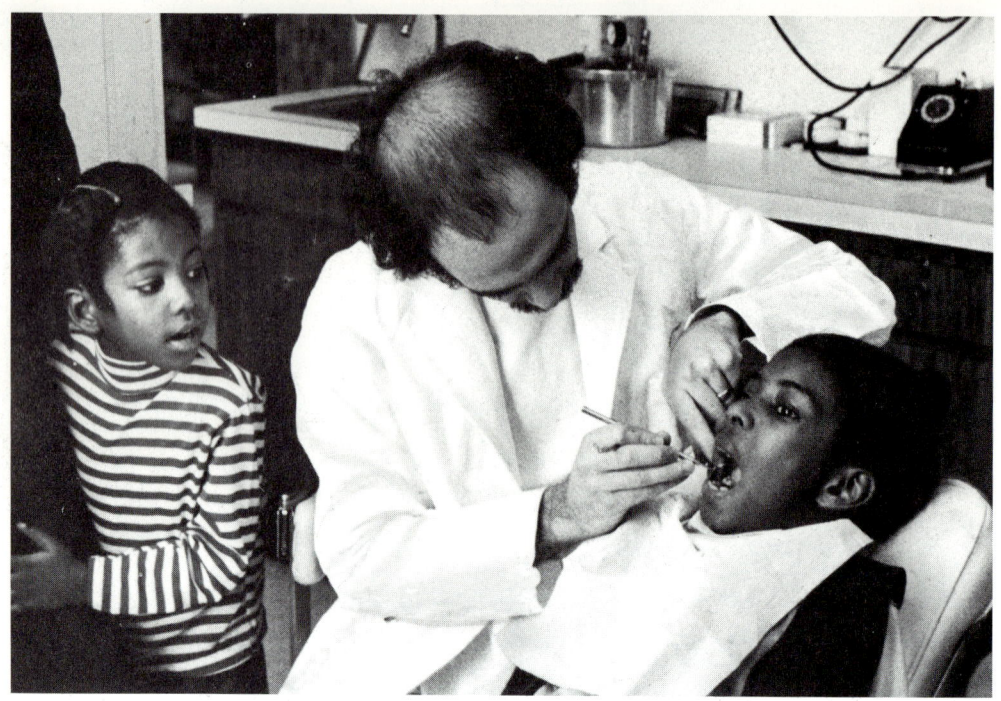

Your Teeth and You

Take care of your teeth and get checkups.

You should visit your dentist at least once a year. The dentist will check your teeth to see if they are growing straight. He or she will check your gums to see if they are firm and pink or light red in color. It is difficult to chew food properly if your teeth are crooked. And soft gums can cause loss of teeth.

The dentist will check to see if your teeth are clean. Are you using *dental floss* (děn′tl flôs′)? Are you brushing the right way? The dentist may find a *cavity* (kăv′ĭ tē), or a hole, in your tooth. If so, he or she will clean out the cavity and fill it with a special material.

Eating too many sweets can cause cavities. So the dentist will remind you that drinking milk and eating cheese help make your teeth strong. And eating fruits and vegetables helps make your gums firm and healthy.

QUESTIONS

1. A *cavity* is a
    a. tooth.
    b. hole.
    c. filling.

2. The dentist should check your teeth
    a. at least once a year.
    b. about once every two years.
    c. every week.

3. According to the story, if your teeth are not growing in straight, you will not
    a. be able to eat any food at all.
    b. have to brush them often.
    c. be able to chew food correctly.

4. In order to have strong teeth and firm gums, you should
    a. eat only fruits and vegetables.
    b. eat the right kinds of food.
    c. drink nothing but milk.

5. The *main idea* of this story is that
    a. the only thing you have to do to have strong teeth is to brush them often.
    b. if you do not eat sweets, you will never have a cavity.
    c. there are many things you must do if you want strong teeth and healthy gums.

Black and White All Over

Do you know who Ling-Ling and Hsing-Hsing are?

In 1972, Ling-Ling and Hsing-Hsing arrived at their new home in the National Zoo in Washington, D.C. Ling-Ling and Hsing-Hsing are *pandas* (păn′dəz) and were gifts from the people of China to the people of the United States.

Pandas live in the forests and mountain areas of China and Tibet. Ling-Ling and Hsing-Hsing are giant pandas. There are two types of pandas, the giant panda and the red panda. Giant pandas are black and white, have short tails, and grow to be about 1 to 1½ meters tall. Some pandas weigh up to 135 kilograms! Because of their size and shape, pandas look very much like bears. They even walk slowly, just like bears. Some scientists believe that the panda is a member of the bear family, but others disagree.

Pandas like to eat bamboo shoots. Bamboo is a plant that grows in China and Tibet. Workers at the zoo want Ling-Ling and Hsing-Hsing to feel at home, so the pandas get lots of bamboo shoots to eat.

QUESTIONS

1. *Panda* is the name given to
    a. an animal that lives in zoos.
    b. an animal found in the forests of China.
    c. all black and white animals.

2. Ling-Ling and Hsing-Hsing
    a. are giant pandas.
    b. are 2 meters tall.
    c. have red fur.

3. The pandas
    a. will return to China soon.
    b. like to eat bamboo shoots.
    c. have very long tails.

4. Which of the following statements is *true?*
    a. Giant pandas may be part of the bear family.
    b. All pandas are black and white.
    c. The zoo workers do not like taking care of the pandas.

5. The story tells us that
    a. there is more than one type of panda.
    b. Ling-Ling and Hsing-Hsing live in Tibet.
    c. giant pandas cannot be kept in zoos.

Meet the Cactus

When are a bunny's ears green? When does a rat's tail grow in a basket?

Was your answer "When it is a cactus plant"? If so, you are right! Plants that belong to the cactus family are special. Cactus plants can live for weeks without being watered. They store extra water in their roots and stems.

The cactus plant is a green plant. Like other green plants, it uses sunlight to make food. It makes its food in its stem. The body of the cactus is usually covered with spines. These spines can be soft and hairy. Or they can be hard and pointed like a needle. Also, all cactus plants have some type of flower.

There are hundreds of different kinds of cactus plants. Some, like the "living rock" cactus, are small and almost round. Others, like the "bunny ears" cactus, can grow quite tall and wide. And still other cactus plants, like the "rattail," grow long, thin stems that hang down.

QUESTIONS

1. A *cactus* is
    a. an animal.
    b. a plant.
    c. a flower.

2. A cactus plant is *special* because it
    a. is tall and wide.
    b. has spines.
    c. can store water.

3. The cactus plant is like other green plants because it
    a. has scratchy spines that are like needles.
    b. has no flowers.
    c. uses sunlight to make its own food.

4. The food is made in the ―――― of the cactus.
    a. stem
    b. spines
    c. roots

5. Cactus plants are good plants to grow in places where
    a. there is a lot of rain.
    b. there is very little rain.
    c. it is always dry.

Sugar Snap Peas

Do you like peas? You will love the "Sugar Snap."

Peas are seeds that we eat as vegetables. Peas are found in long green cases called *pods* (pŏdz). These pods, or seed cases, grow on a vine.

Scientists, like Dr. Calvin Lamborn, are always looking for ways to grow better, tastier vegetables. For years, Dr. Lamborn tested many different kinds of seeds. He wanted to grow a better pea. And he succeeded in growing the Sugar Snap pea.

The Sugar Snap is a different kind of pea. You can eat all of it—both the pea and the pod. Usually, a pea pod is tough, and people throw it away. But the Sugar Snap pod is tasty and good to eat. Also, Sugar Snap peas have a wonderful, sweet flavor.

The first seeds for this new pea were sold in 1979. Now, Sugar Snaps are growing in many gardens. People like to pick them from the vine and eat them raw. They say that is when the Sugar Snap tastes the sweetest.

QUESTIONS

1. A *pod* is
    a. a seed case.
    b. a vine.
    c. a kind of pea.

2. Peas are eaten as
    a. candies.
    b. vegetables.
    c. seeds.

3. One reason the Sugar Snap pea is different from most other peas is that
    a. the pod is good to eat.
    b. it does not grow on a vine.
    c. it is not a seed.

4. Why do you think these new peas are called Sugar Snaps?
    a. They have a sweet taste.
    b. They taste sweetest when they are cooked.
    c. They can be used to make sugar.

5. The *main idea* of this story is that
    a. scientists are always looking for ways to grow better foods.
    b. pea pods are not eaten because they are tough and tasteless.
    c. Sugar Snap peas are growing in many gardens.

The Ginkgo Tree

The ginkgo is called a "living fossil."

 Ginkgoes (gĭng′kōz) are a kind of tree. The ginkgo tree has dark, waxy leaves that look something like a fan. The leaves of the ginkgo help to give the tree its full shape.

 Ginkgoes have grown on Earth since the time of the dinosaur. We know this because leaves from the ginkgo have been found as *fossils* (fŏs′əlz). Fossils are the remains, or what is left, of plants and animals that lived long ago. They are found in certain kinds of rock. The ginkgo fossils have the same shape as the leaves you see on the ginkgo tree today. The ginkgo's leaves have not changed a bit.

 Ginkgoes grow well almost everywhere in North America. They can grow where most other trees cannot. So people are planting ginkgo trees along city streets. Even city smoke and soot do not seem to bother them. No wonder the ginkgo tree has been around for such a long time.

QUESTIONS

1. The remains of plants and animals that lived long ago are called
    a. rocks.
    b. fossils.
    c. leaves.

2. The leaves of the ginkgo
    a. are dark and fan-shaped.
    b. are light green in color.
    c. make the tree look tall and thin.

3. Fossils of ginkgo leaves
    a. prove that the ginkgo is not very old.
    b. have been found in certain kinds of rocks.
    c. do not look very much like ginkgo leaves today.

4. After reading the story, which statement would you say *best* describes the ginkgo?
    a. Ginkgoes have long, pointed leaves.
    b. The ginkgo has been growing on Earth for millions of years.
    c. The ginkgo cannot live in cities where the air is dirty.

5. Which of the following words tells you what a ginkgo is?
    a. fossil
    b. rock
    c. tree

PEOPLE TO KNOW

Dr. Jane Wright

Dr. Jane Wright was born on November 30, 1919. Her father was Dr. Louis Tompkins Wright. Louis Tompkins Wright was a famous civil rights leader and cancer researcher. Cancer is a disease that destroys human cells.

When Jane Wright was very young, she wanted to be an artist. But everyone in her family since her great-great-grandfather had been a doctor. So she changed her mind. Jane Wright decided that she, too, would study to become a doctor.

Dr. Wright attended Smith College in Massachusetts. She received a degree in medicine from New York Medical College. Dr. Wright was an excellent student. In addition, she was an outstanding swimmer and was a member of the varsity swimming team.

Today, Dr. Wright is a leader in the field of cancer research. She has directed several cancer research projects. As a result of her work, Dr. Wright has discovered drug treatments for certain kinds of cancer.

PLACES TO GO

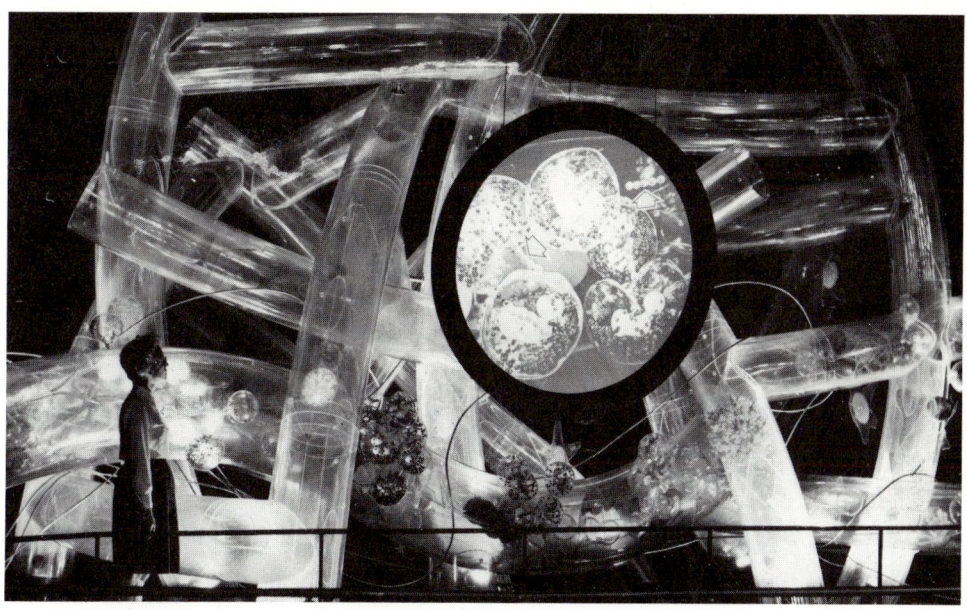

A Visit to the Cleveland Health Education Museum

See your heart beat. Test how strong your lungs are. Find out how your eyes work. These are some of the things you can do at the Cleveland Health Education Museum. The museum is in Cleveland, Ohio. It is the only one of its kind in the world.

Each year, many people visit the museum. They learn how the human body works and how to take care of it.

The museum has many exhibits. In the Theater of Vision, you can walk into the center of the human eye. In this exhibit, you can learn how your eye is made and how it works. In the Theater of Hearing, you explore the wonders of how you hear. In the Kahn Hall, you see giant models of fungus, mold, and bacteria. And you can look through a microscope to see fungus, bacteria, and mold. The museum also has a walk-in tooth.

PUZZLES TO DO

Animals of North America

Find the names of some common animals that live in North America. The names of the animals go across and down. When you find a name, circle it. The names of the animals are: EARTHWORM   BEAVER   FROG   SQUIRREL   BEAR   TURTLE   ANT   CROW   GRASSHOPPER   BUTTERFLY   PORCUPINE   SNAIL   RAT   TROUT   SALMON   WOLF   COYOTE   FOX   BAT   DEER   EAGLE   MOOSE   SPIDER   SNAKE   ROBIN   ALLIGATOR   RACCOON   MOUNTAIN LION

```
O M O O G E A G G E L S L
F O X I R A C P O N S Q I
R U A S A L M O N A N U R
O N P N S O C T O B A T A
G T O S S Q R U R E D R C
E A R T H W O R M A I M C
A I C I O S W T S V L O O
G N U D P N A L N E S O O
L L P E P A B E A R T S N
E I I R E K U R I T R E U
A O N T R U T E L R A C S
G N E B E A T R O U T O P
S Q U I R R E L I O A R I
N U I D E E R O B I N W D
A I R W O L F N A T T T E
K P O R A L L I G A T O R
E P O R C O Y O T E D E R
```

Insects

Fill in the spaces with the names of 11 insects that are listed below.

4-Letter Words

bees
ants
lice

5-Letter Words

wasps
moths

6-Letter Word

aphids

7-Letter Word

beetles

8-Letter Words

mayflies
crickets
termites

9-Letter Word

fireflies

SCIENCE ADVENTURES

A Food Record

Food is important to help us live and grow. We need food to help us work and play. We need food to help us stay healthy. We need food to help make our teeth and bones strong.

We should eat some of each of these foods every day:

Fruits and Vegetables

Dairy Foods

Grains

Meat and Poultry

Keep a record of the foods you eat each day for three days.

Compare your food record with others in your class.

THREE-DAY FOOD RECORD

Day: Date:			
Fruits and Vegetables			
Dairy Foods			
Grains			
Meat and Poultry			
Soda, Candy, and Other "Junk Food"			

EARTH-SPACE SCIENCE

Jupiter is the largest planet in the solar system. Cameras on Voyager I took photographs of the planet and four of its moons. Later, the photographs were combined to make this picture. It does not show the right size of the moons. But it shows the right positions. Io (upper left) is the closest moon. Europa is in the center. Then comes Ganymede. Finally, you can see Callisto in the right-hand corner. Jupiter has nine other, smaller moons.

A Deadly Dinosaur

Some old animal bones were found in 1964.

Dinosaurs (dī′nə sôrz′) were animals that lived long ago. Dinosaur bones have been found in many places. But the dinosaur bones found in Montana in 1964 were different from any found before.

While scientists were putting the bones found in Montana together, they discovered many things. This dinosaur once stood about 135 centimeters tall and weighed about 72 kilograms. It walked on its back legs and could run like a large bird. Also, it had a long tail that helped it move quickly and easily.

Scientists were surprised to discover that this dinosaur had feet with sharp, pointed claws about 10 centimeters long. So the dinosaur was named *Deinonychus* (dī′nə nĭk′əs), which means "terrible claw." Deinonychus probably used its claws for protection and for hunting.

Scientists believe Deinonychus hunted in packs, or groups. For this reason, these dinosaurs were not afraid to hunt much larger animals for food. Also, its sharp claws made Deinonychus a deadly dinosaur.

QUESTIONS

1. The name *Deinonychus* means
    a. deadly.
    b. terrible claw.
    c. dinosaur bones.

2. The bones found in Montana in 1964 were
    a. different from other dinosaur bones.
    b. from a very large bird.
    c. like any other animal bones.

3. Why was Deinonychus a "deadly dinosaur"?
    a. because of its long, sharp claws
    b. because it had a long tail
    c. because it was about 135 centimeters tall

4. Scientists believe that Deinonychus probably
    a. did not eat meat.
    b. hunted with other dinosaurs.
    c. found it difficult to move quickly.

5. In the story, which of the following things happened *first?*
    a. The dinosaur was named Deinonychus.
    b. Scientists began putting the dinosaur bones together.
    c. Scientists discovered that Deinonychus walked on its back legs.

A Black Graveyard for Animals

What are the La Brea Tar Pits?

Over a hundred years ago, Henry Hancock owned a ranch in California. There were sticky, black tar pits on the land. They smelled like oil and gas. The pits were named the La Brea Tar Pits.

Mr. Hancock decided to sell the tar to some road builders. But the workers were surprised when they began to dig. The tar was full of old bones! Many of the bones were of animals that were *extinct* (ĭk stĭngkt′), or had disappeared from Earth, a long time ago. Some of these extinct animals were a giant bird, a "short-faced" bear, a tiny horse, and a saber-toothed tiger.

One day, someone discovered how the animals had been trapped in the pits. A man was watching the shiny pools of tar. He saw a duck try to get a drink from a tar pit. But it got stuck in the bubbling tar and cried out. Hungry animals heard the duck and got stuck trying to catch it. Over thousands of years, many animals died this way.

QUESTIONS

1. Something that disappeared from Earth a long time ago is
    a. trapped.
    b. extinct.
    c. discovered.

2. What did the tar pits smell like?
    a. oil and gas
    b. drinking water
    c. ranch animals

3. According to the story, tar can be used in making
    a. roads.
    b. oil and gas.
    c. paint.

4. What did the animals sometimes think the tar pits looked like?
    a. something good to eat
    b. old bones
    c. drinking water

5. Why did other animals get stuck after the duck got stuck?
    a. They were after a meal.
    b. They tried to help the duck.
    c. They were afraid.

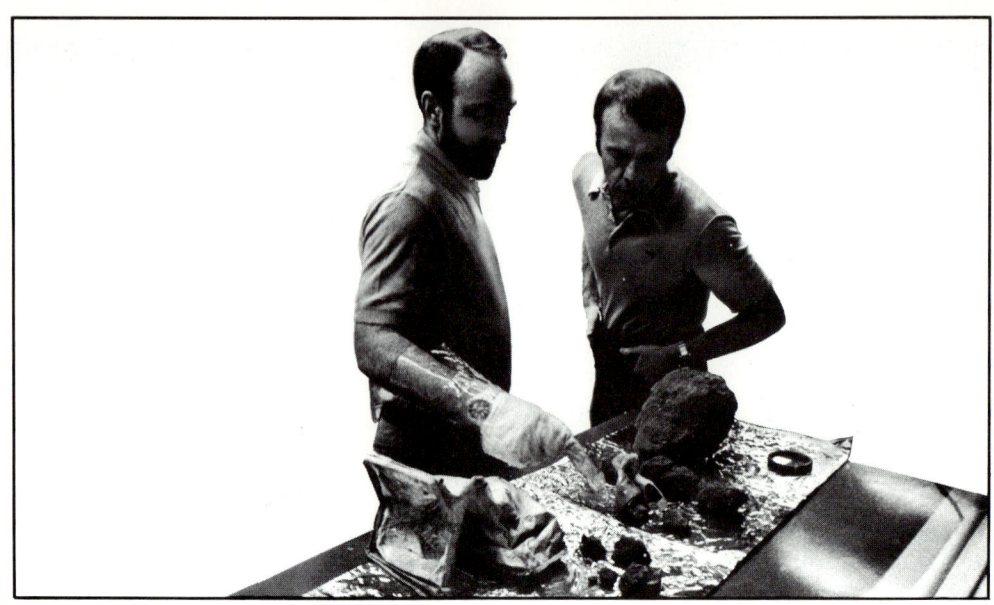

Moon Rocks Tell Many Secrets

We are learning about the moon from its rocks.

People have always wondered about the moon. When and how was it formed? Was there life on the moon? Was the moon like Earth? No one knew. Then, between 1969 and 1972, there were ten moon landings by American *astronauts* (ăs′trə nôts′). An astronaut is a person who travels into space. The astronauts brought back samples of moon rocks each time they landed.

Scientists have learned many things by studying these rocks. They have learned that there was probably never any life on the moon. Also, it seems likely that Earth and the moon formed at about the same time. But the rocks do not tell how the moon and Earth were formed.

Moon rocks show that for a long time, Earth and the moon changed in the same way. Then, about 3 billion years ago, they began to change in different ways. By studying the rocks, scientists can tell when this happened but not why. The moon still holds many secrets.

QUESTIONS

1. An *astronaut* is
   - a. a person who travels into space.
   - b. one kind of rock found on the moon.
   - c. something that lives on the moon.

2. The moon rocks show that there
   - a. is life on the moon now.
   - b. was probably never any life on the moon.
   - c. was life on the moon over 3 billion years ago.

3. The moon rocks show us _____ the moon and Earth were formed.
   - a. when
   - b. how
   - c. why

4. The secrets we have learned from the moon's rocks tell us
   - a. what is happening on Earth now.
   - b. what has happened on the moon in the past.
   - c. what will happen on the moon in years to come.

5. According to the story, which of the following is *true?*
   - a. There are many things yet to be learned about the moon.
   - b. By studying the moon rocks, scientists have learned all of the moon's secrets.
   - c. Studying the moon rocks helped scientists learn why the moon changed.

Is There Life on Mars?

Could there be green plants on Mars?

There was a time when people told stories and made jokes about little green men who lived on Mars. Today, we know there are no little green men on Mars. But some scientists believe that there may be some kind of green plant growing there.

Mars has seasons like those on Earth. But each season on Mars is longer than an Earth season. Mars takes 687 days to move around the sun—almost twice as long as Earth takes. This means that a season on Mars lasts for nearly 6 Earth months.

Pictures of Mars show a change of color as the seasons change there. Some scientists believe this color change may be caused by plants that grow thick as the seasons turn warm. Other scientists believe the color change may be caused by giant dust storms. We will not know which scientists are right until the day we land on Mars.

QUESTIONS

1. Mars has ———— like those on Earth.
    - a. summers
    - b. winters
    - c. seasons

2. On Mars, a season lasts for nearly
    - a. 2 months.
    - b. 6 months.
    - c. 2 years.

3. It takes Mars ———— it takes Earth to move around the sun.
    - a. the same time as
    - b. almost twice as long as
    - c. a much shorter time than

4. The change of color on Mars may be caused by
    - a. giant dust storms.
    - b. spacecraft landing on Mars.
    - c. the short seasons on Mars.

5. Which of the following statements is *true?*
    - a. There is no life on Mars.
    - b. Scientists agree that we will never be able to land on Mars.
    - c. There are many questions still to be answered about Mars.

Hurricane Watch

Pilots fly right into a hurricane? Why?

Hurricanes (hûr′ĭ kānz′) are big storms that start over water and bring strong winds. Hurricane winds can blow at 120 kilometers per hour or more and must be watched.

Who watches a hurricane? Hurricane hunters do. They are weather scientists who fly into a hurricane in an airplane.

Inside the plane, there are many instruments that the hurricane hunters use to find out things about the hurricane. What kind of information are these weather scientists looking for?

For one thing, hurricane hunters need to know where the hurricane is moving. So they use the instruments to track the storm. If it starts moving towards land, they send out warnings. Then, people can move out of the way before the hurricane hits. These hurricane hunters help save many lives.

QUESTIONS

1. A *hurricane* is a
    a. big storm with strong winds.
    b. kind of airplane.
    c. wind instrument.

2. Hurricanes start
    a. in the mountains.
    b. on land.
    c. over water.

3. Which of the following statements is *not* true?
    a. Hurricane hunters are weather scientists.
    b. Hurricane hunters use instruments to track storms.
    c. Hurricane hunters do most of their work on the ground.

4. According to the story, hurricane hunters watch a storm from
    a. an airplane.
    b. a tracking station.
    c. a boat.

5. Hurricane hunters are important because they
    a. are able to stop storms.
    b. warn people when storms are coming.
    c. know how to fly airplanes.

Cool, Clear Water

Icebergs may be a source of fresh water.

Do you know how important fresh water is? Count the number of times you use water in one day. Water is used for drinking, washing, and growing foods.

Some countries are located in very dry, or *arid* (ăr′ĭd), areas. That is, people in those countries do not have much water for drinking and growing food. But one of these arid countries is planning a new way to get more fresh water. It wants to get water from icebergs!

An iceberg is a large block of floating ice that has broken away from a glacier. A *glacier* (glā′shər) is a large body of slowly moving ice. Glaciers are found in very cold places. Icebergs can be several kilometers long and several hundred meters thick. They contain mostly fresh-water ice. Tugboats could tow the icebergs from cold places to the arid areas. Part of the iceberg would melt along the way. But enough of the iceberg would be left to be used as water.

QUESTIONS

1. The word *arid* means
    a. ice.
    b. dry.
    c. thick.

2. An iceberg
    a. does not move.
    b. can be several kilometers long.
    c. is usually found in arid countries.

3. Fresh water is used
    a. to build icebergs.
    b. now and then.
    c. for drinking and washing.

4. The *main idea* of the second paragraph is that
    a. people are finding new ways to get fresh water.
    b. arid countries have more water than they need.
    c. water for growing food is easy to find.

5. If arid countries cannot find a way to get more fresh water,
    a. they will not be able to use glacier water for drinking.
    b. they may not be able to grow enough food for their people.
    c. there will be fewer icebergs.

Mountains of Ice

Icebergs can be dangerous.

It is April in the North Atlantic Ocean. Suddenly, there is a sound like thunder. A giant block of ice breaks off from a *glacier* (glā′shər). An iceberg is born.

Berg is a German word for "mountain." An iceberg is like a mountain of ice rising above the water. But the part of the iceberg that is above the water is only a small part of the whole thing. Most of the iceberg is underwater and cannot be seen. The bottom of a ship could be torn open if it hit this hidden part of an iceberg.

The United States Coast Guard uses planes and ships to watch the waters where icebergs are usually found. The Coast Guard also keeps track of the iceberg when it is spotted. Then, the Coast Guard can warn ships to steer around it. These iceberg watchers have helped save many ships and many lives.

QUESTIONS

1. The German word for "mountain" is
    a. kilometer.
    b. thunder.
    c. berg.

2. Most of the iceberg is usually
    a. above the water.
    b. made of salt.
    c. under the water.

3. An iceberg is dangerous because
    a. most of it is hidden.
    b. it breaks off from a glacier.
    c. it looks like a mountain.

4. When ships see an iceberg, they
    a. must return to shore.
    b. go around it.
    c. push it away.

5. The United States Coast Guard helps save ships and lives by
    a. tracking icebergs and warning ships.
    b. melting the tops of icebergs.
    c. steering icebergs out of the ships' way.

All Aboard the *Alvin*

A tiny ship takes scientists deep into the sea.

The *Alvin* is a deep-diving *submersible* (səb mûr′sə bəl). A submersible can be used to travel under water. Scientists use this small submersible to study the deep sea. Let's join one of those scientists now. Let's climb aboard the *Alvin*.

Down we dive, deep into the sea. Soon, the *Alvin* is more than 2 kilometers deep. The water temperature is near freezing at this level. But we are warm and comfortable inside the *Alvin*.

The sea around us is completely dark now. So the *Alvin*'s pilot turns on the ship's big headlights. Then, the cameras on board begin taking pictures of the sea floor.

The *Alvin* has three windows. As we look out the windows, the scientist pushes a button. We see a long hook come out from the ship. It scoops up samples of rocks, minerals, and dirt from the sea floor. Later, scientists will study these samples to learn more about this world under the sea.

QUESTIONS

1. If something is *submersible*, it
    a. can take pictures.
    b. can go under water.
    c. has more than two windows.

2. A scientist would use the *Alvin* mainly to
    a. study the deep parts of the sea.
    b. travel from one place to another.
    c. learn how to dive in the deep sea.

3. When the *Alvin* is 2 kilometers deep, the
    a. people on board are uncomfortable.
    b. water temperature is about freezing.
    c. inside of the ship becomes very cold.

4. Why does the *Alvin* have headlights?
    a. so people on the ship can see each other
    b. so scientists can look at the sea floor
    c. so the pilot can see which button to push

5. In the story, which of the following happens *last?*
    a. The sea becomes very dark and cold.
    b. Cameras on the *Alvin* take pictures of the sea floor.
    c. Samples of rocks are taken from the sea floor.

PEOPLE TO KNOW

Jacques Cousteau

What human spends more time in the sea than on the land? Who swims side by side with sharks, mantas, and seals? Who has hitchhiked a ride on a giant tortoise? Why, it's Jacques Cousteau, of course!

Jacques Cousteau is one of the inventors of the *Aqua-lung* (ăk'wə lŭng'). The Aqua-lung lets people breathe under the water. After testing his Aqua-lung, Cousteau said, "I stood upside down on one finger . . . I flew about in space . . ."

The space Cousteau spoke about was the never-ending space under the sea. This world under the sea makes up the largest part of our Earth. Cousteau first began exploring the sea in the 1940s. Since then, he has explored ice formations in the Antarctic. And he has looked for treasure in sunken ships. He also has written books about the Coral Sea, whales, and dolphins. And Jacques Cousteau has brought the undersea world to millions of people through the lenses of underwater television cameras.

PLACES TO GO

A Visit to the Alabama Space and Rocket Center

Do you know who monkeynaut Baker is? You can find out who she is. All you have to do is visit the Alabama Space and Rocket Center in Huntsville, Alabama. It is the world's largest space museum.

Monkeynaut Baker is a tiny squirrel monkey that lives at the space center. Baker made space history in 1959. She was the first monkey to travel into outer space and return safely.

On May 28, 1959, scientists placed the little 1-pound monkey aboard a rocket. The rocket traveled more than 480 kilometers into space. The trip ended with a splashdown in the Atlantic Ocean. Baker was safe. Her trip paved the way for space flights by humans.

Baker is one of the most popular exhibits at the space center. She lives in a special cage that has a water fountain and a trapeze. Her favorite foods are oranges, hard-boiled eggs, and, of course, bananas.

PUZZLES TO DO

The Earth

How much do you know about the earth? Hidden in the mountain are 12 words that relate to the earth. The words go across, down, and diagonally. Use the list of words below for help.

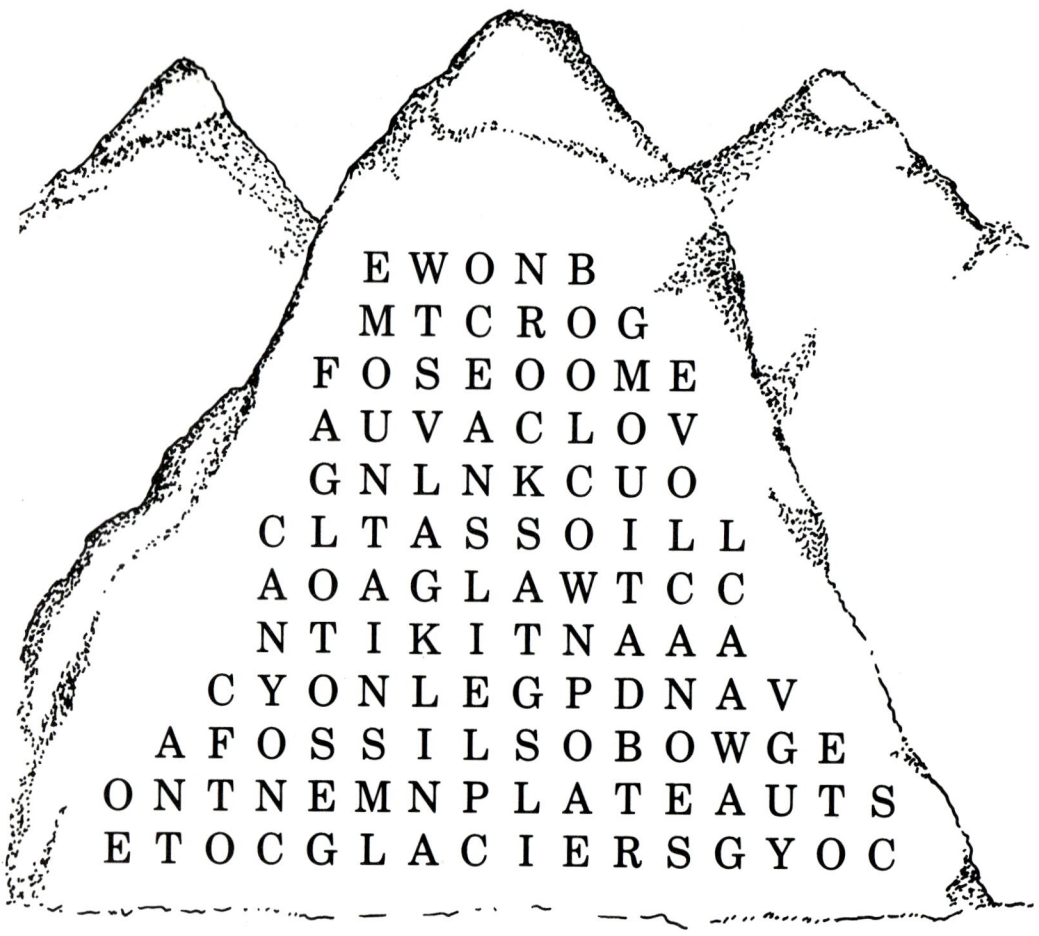

```
      E W O N B
      M T C R O G
      F O S E O O M E
      A U V A C L O V
      G N L N K C U O
    C L T A S S O I L L
    A O A G L A W T C C
    N T I K I T N A A A
    C Y O N L E G P D N A V
   A F O S S I L S O B O W G E
   O N T N E M N P L A T E A U T S
   E T O C G L A C I E R S G Y O C
```

Word List

SOIL ROCKS OCEANS GLACIERS VOLCANOES
MOUNTAINS FOSSILS CAVES LAKES CANYON
PLATEAU SAND

68

Weather

Can you solve the crossword puzzle? If you need help, use the words below.

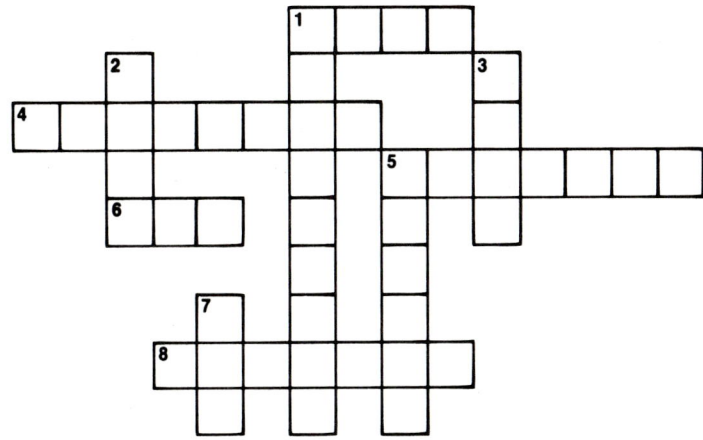

Across

1. small frozen raindrops
4. heavy snowstorm
5. average weather conditions in a place over a long period of time
6. water vapor that condenses on a surface
8. large, whirling storm that occurs mostly over land

Down

1. large storm with strong winds and rain
2. moving air
3. water falling in drops
5. water particles light enough to float
7. cloud that can touch the ground

Word List

hurricane   tornado   blizzard   hail   climate   rain   clouds   fog   wind   dew

SCIENCE ADVENTURES

A Weather Record

Weather affects the clothes you wear.
Weather affects what you do.
It even affects the way you feel.

Weather can be described in different ways.

Temperature is measured in units called degrees (°).

Clouds, wind, and other aspects of the weather can also be described.

We can use the symbols on this page to make a record of the weather.

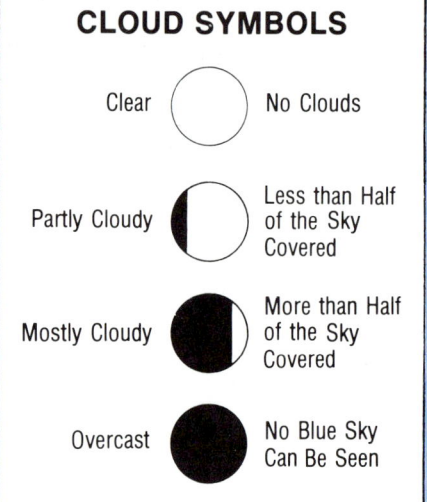

CLOUD SYMBOLS

- Clear — No Clouds
- Partly Cloudy — Less than Half of the Sky Covered
- Mostly Cloudy — More than Half of the Sky Covered
- Overcast — No Blue Sky Can Be Seen

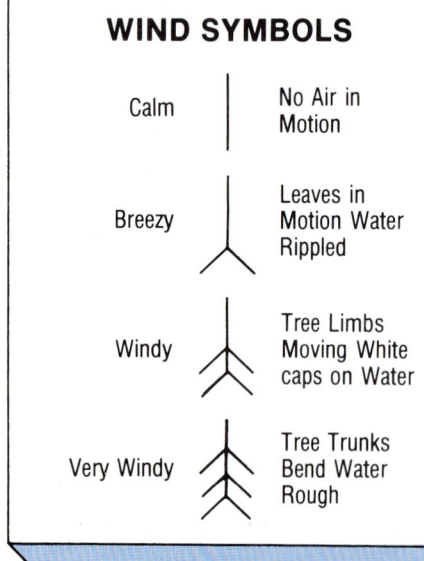

WIND SYMBOLS

- Calm — No Air in Motion
- Breezy — Leaves in Motion Water Rippled
- Windy — Tree Limbs Moving White caps on Water
- Very Windy — Tree Trunks Bend Water Rough

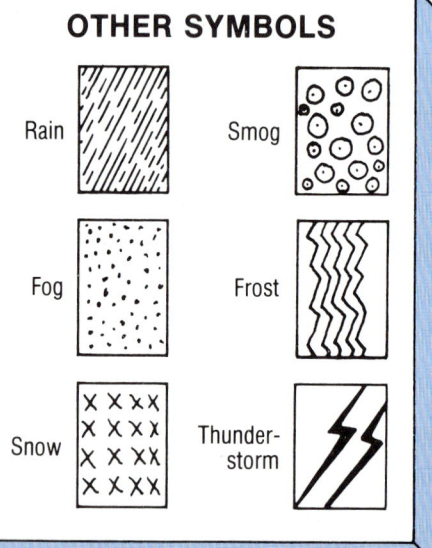

OTHER SYMBOLS

- Rain
- Smog
- Fog
- Frost
- Snow
- Thunderstorm

Keep a record of the weather for several weeks.
Make your observations at the same time each day.

WEATHER CHART

Day	Date	Temperature	Clouds	Wind	Other
Mon.					
Tue.					
Wed.					
Thur.					
Fri.					
Mon.					
Tue.					
Wed.					
Thur.					
Fri.					
Mon.					
Tue.					
Wed.					
Thur.					
Fri.					

PHYSICAL SCIENCE

Up, up, and away! These people are going for a ride in a hot-air balloon. The air inside the balloon is being warmed by the small heater under the balloon's opening. When the balloon is full of warm air, it will rise. It will lift the basket and the people high into the air. How do you think they will get down?

Hang Gliding

Would you like to ride the winds in a large kite?

Did you know that people can soar and float in the wind? Well, they can. They use hang gliders. Hang gliders are like large kites.

The person who rides a hang glider is called a pilot. The pilot holds on to the hang glider and runs down a hill. The hang glider lifts off into the air. The pilot rides in a seat under the glider.

In the air, the pilot uses a control stick to steer the glider up, down, and from side to side. The pilot tries to find a thermal. A *thermal* (thûr′məl) is a wave of rising hot air. The rising hot air keeps the glider up. Mountain areas are good places to find thermals.

Hawaii is one good place to go hang gliding. The winds are strong, and there are good thermals. One pilot was able to hang glide in the air for over 12 hours!

QUESTIONS

1. A wave of rising hot air is called
    a. a glider.
    b. a thermal.
    c. a kite.

2. In this story, a pilot is someone who
    a. rides a hang glider.
    b. makes large kites.
    c. lives in Hawaii.

3. A control stick is used to
    a. keep a hang glider on the ground.
    b. hold the pilot in his or her seat.
    c. steer a hang glider up, down, and sideways.

4. Why is a thermal important in hang gliding?
    a. It keeps the glider up in the air.
    b. It makes the air warm.
    c. The pilot uses it to hang on to the glider.

5. If you wanted to hang glide, you would go to a place where
    a. the air is cold.
    b. the winds are light.
    c. the thermals are good.

Hot-Air Balloon

How does a hot-air balloon work?

Many years ago, in 1783, two Frenchmen found out that a paper bag filled with hot air will float. From this discovery came the idea that people might be able to travel by hot-air balloons. People simply made giant paper bags and got into a basket hooked to the bottom of the bag. Next, they filled the bag with hot air, and up they went! People used to burn straw to keep the air inside the balloon hot.

Today, hot-air ballooning is different from what it was in those early times. Now, the balloons are made of nylon, not paper. Today, balloonists use a gas burner to keep the air hot. But ballooning is still just as exciting.

Once off the ground, balloonists are in for a breathtaking ride. Except for the sound of the gas burner, the ride is quiet. No wind is felt, since the balloon travels with the wind. Finally, the balloonist turns down the gas burner. The air in the balloon cools, and the balloon floats back to the ground.

QUESTIONS

1. A *balloon* is a
    a. special kind of gas.
    b. bag filled with air.
    c. basket hooked to a bag.

2. No wind is felt on a balloon ride, because
    a. the balloon travels with the wind.
    b. the people are inside the balloon.
    c. the distance traveled is not great.

3. To come back to the ground, the balloonist
    a. throws the gas burner out of the balloon.
    b. lets air out of the balloon.
    c. turns down the gas burner.

4. The balloons in this story work because
    a. people steer them.
    b. hot air rises.
    c. cold air is light.

5. Traveling in a balloon is probably most like
    a. flying in an airplane.
    b. riding in a car.
    c. floating on a cloud.

Sailboats Go Back to Work

We may be seeing many more sails on the sea.

Once, the wind powered most ships that traveled the seas. The wind pushed against the ship's sails. And the ship moved across the water. Then, other ways were found to power ships. And sailboats were no longer work boats. They became boats for fun.

Now, sailboats may be put back to work. This is because the wind is free. The oil that drives our modern ships is *not* free. In fact, the cost of oil is going up. Yet both wind and oil have *energy* (ĕn′ər jē). Energy is the push needed to do work.

Hold your hand into the wind and you can feel the push of the wind's energy. Oil's energy cannot be felt easily. Oil must be burned before its energy can be used.

The new sailboats would have sails just like the old ones. But new ways to move the sails would be used. The sailor would push a button to turn a sail instead of pulling on a thick rope. Also, sailors would use new ways to find the best winds and to watch out for bad weather.

QUESTIONS

1. To do work, you need
    a. oil.
    b. energy.
    c. a rope.

2. Wind and oil
    a. burn energy.
    b. cost a lot.
    c. have energy.

3. Sailboats may be put to work because
    a. wind is free.
    b. they are fun.
    c. no energy is needed to run them.

4. A sailboat moves across the water when
    a. the sailor pushes a button.
    b. the wind pushes the boat.
    c. the wind pushes the sail.

5. The story states that one way to make sailing a boat easier is to use new ways to
    a. find the best winds.
    b. make energy last longer.
    c. burn oil when it is needed.

What Do You Think?

Noise is all around us.

When you see the word *dangerous* (dān'jər əs), what do you think about? Fire? Guns? Broken glass? How about noise? Can noise be dangerous? Can it hurt you?

Most people would say that noise is loud, unwanted sound. They think of the roar of traffic, the scream of jet planes, and the howl of a sick animal. But what about rock music? Is the sound of music noise?

Sounds can be measured to find out how loud they are. Your hearing can also be measured. Tests were done on people who work with very loud machines for a long time. The tests showed that some of these people had a loss of hearing. People who race cars, fly jet planes, or play in rock bands may also have hearing problems.

Tests also show other changes in people who must be in loud, noisy places. These changes can take place in the way people breathe or see or think or move or feel. Can noise be *dangerous*? What do you think?

QUESTIONS

1. To test a sound, we must
    a. change it.
    b. measure it.
    c. time it.

2. Tests show a loss of hearing in people who
    a. measure loud sounds.
    b. play rock music on their radios.
    c. work with very loud machines for a long time.

3. Which of the following can be dangerous?
    a. all sounds
    b. most sounds
    c. very loud sounds

4. Another name for this story could be
    a. "Sounds Can Be Measured."
    b. "Noise Can Be Dangerous."
    c. "How to Test Your Hearing."

5. People who fly jet planes may have hearing problems. One reason may be that jets
    a. fly too fast.
    b. fly too high above the ground.
    c. make a loud noise on takeoff and landing.

How a Battery Works

Many new games and tools work on batteries.

A *battery* (băt′ə rē) is made up of one or more cells. The cells are used to make electricity. One kind of battery is the D-cell battery. D-cell batteries are small. So they can be used in such things as flashlights, clocks, electric games, and tape recorders.

One kind of D-cell is made up of a zinc case. There is a rod of black material called carbon in the middle of the case. The rest of the cell is filled with a *chemical* (kĕm′ĭ kəl) paste. The zinc and the carbon have to be connected in some way in order for the cells in the battery to make electricity. Then, electricity flows, and the toy or flashlight works.

The D-cell battery stops working when the zinc wears out or the chemical paste is used up. Your toy or tool will stop working when this happens. Then, it is time to buy a new battery.

QUESTIONS

1. A *battery* is _____ used to produce electricity.
    a. a kind of electric wire
    b. made up of one or more cells
    c. a special chemical

2. The D-cell is
    a. used mainly in cars.
    b. used only in flashlights.
    c. a small battery.

3. The black material in the center of a D-cell may be
    a. carbon.
    b. zinc.
    c. paste.

4. In order for the cells in a battery to make electricity, there *must* be a connection between
    a. the zinc and the carbon.
    b. the paste and the battery.
    c. the carbon and the toy or tool.

5. If a battery-powered game stopped working, it could be that
    a. the rod was made of carbon.
    b. there were chemicals in the paste.
    c. the zinc wore out.

Solar Heat

The future of solar heating looks very bright.

The heat we get from the sun is called *solar* (sō′lər) heat. Solar heat can be used to heat water and the inside of houses. The picture above shows one kind of solar-heated house.

First, panels are placed on the roof of the house. Each panel is a *collector* (kə lĕk′tər). The collector traps the sun's heat. Water flows through the panels and is heated. Then, the heated water flows through pipes in the house and heats the house.

But cloud cover can cause problems. When the sun is hidden by clouds, the panels cannot collect heat. If too many days go by with no sunshine, there may be no heat or hot water. For this reason, people who use solar heat usually have a "back-up" system, or another way of heating their house.

QUESTIONS

1. The word *solar* means of or by the
    a. air.
    b. sun.
    c. heat.

2. In the story, the panels on the roof of the house
    a. are put on last.
    b. trap water.
    c. collect the sun's heat.

3. As the water flows through the panels, it
    a. is trapped inside them.
    b. cools off the house.
    c. is heated by the sun.

4. How does cloud cover affect a solar-heating system?
    a. The solar collectors cannot trap the sun's heat.
    b. The water will not flow through the pipes in the house.
    c. The solar panels are not able to trap hot water.

5. Which of the following things happens *first?*
    a. Water flows through the panels.
    b. The house is heated.
    c. The collector traps solar heat.

Fuel for Tomorrow

Can cars run without gasoline?

A *fuel* (fyōō′əl) is a substance that can be burned to make energy. Today, gasoline is used as a fuel for cars and airplanes. Tomorrow, we may use different fuels.

One idea is to use old fuels in new ways. *Hydrogen* (hī′drə jən), a kind of gas, is an old fuel. It powers spaceships, and it can power cars and airplanes, too. There are some advantages to using hydrogen. Hydrogen is not as heavy as gasoline, and it is safer. It does not explode as easily. Also, when hydrogen burns, nothing dirty gets into the air.

There are problems, however. Hydrogen gas takes up a lot of space. Cars and airplanes would need bigger fuel tanks. But scientists think they can solve the space problem. They hope that safe, clean hydrogen will be a fuel for tomorrow.

QUESTIONS

1. The word *fuel* is used for anything that
    a. can be burned to make energy.
    b. is put into a tank.
    c. is expensive to burn.

2. According to the story, hydrogen is _____ than gasoline.
    a. dirtier
    b. safer
    c. heavier

3. According to the story, one of the problems with using hydrogen for fuel is that hydrogen gas
    a. takes up a lot of space.
    b. is hard to find.
    c. does not burn very easily.

4. In the story, hydrogen is called an *old fuel* because it has been
    a. used often before.
    b. used in cars for many years.
    c. stored for a long time.

5. Suppose your car used hydrogen gas. Which one of the following statements is the *best* reason for getting a larger fuel tank?
    a. You would not have to refuel so often.
    b. The extra hydrogen would help make the car heavier.
    c. You would burn less of the hydrogen.

87

The Uses of Petroleum

Why is petroleum so important to us?

Do you read at night, or watch TV, or listen to the radio? If you do, you are using some form of *electrical power* (ĭ lĕk′trĭ kəl pou′ər).

Much of the electrical power in this country is made by burning *petroleum* (pə trō′lē əm).

Petroleum means "rock oil," and it comes from deep in the ground. Cars, trucks, planes, and buses burn some form of petroleum as *fuel* (fyo͞o′əl). Fuel is a material that is burned to make heat or power. The light, heat, and power used in many homes come from burning petroleum.

We also use petroleum for many other things. Petroleum is used to make paint, tires, plastics, safety glass, face creams, movie film, shampoo, and hundreds of other things that we all use each day.

Perhaps, in the future, scientists will find another material to take the place of petroleum. Until then, petroleum is very important to us.

QUESTIONS

1. The word *petroleum* means
    a. power.
    b. rock oil.
    c. fuel oil.

2. We get power from petroleum by
    a. burning it.
    b. storing it.
    c. digging for it.

3. Cars, trucks, planes, and buses all burn some form of petroleum as
    a. oil.
    b. fuel.
    c. heat.

4. What is the *main idea* of this story?
    a. Some of the electrical power used in this country comes from burning petroleum.
    b. Cars burn some form of petroleum as fuel.
    c. Without petroleum, we would have to change the way we live.

5. "The Uses of Petroleum" might also have been called
    a. "Making Paint and Plastics from Petroleum."
    b. "How We Heat Our Homes with Petroleum".
    c. "Petroleum: A Very Special Kind of Material."

PEOPLE TO KNOW

Wind Power for School Lights

Some fifth-graders and sixth-graders in Oregon built a windmill. It was a very special windmill. Why? It helped turn on their classroom lights!

The students did all the work, themselves. They even made the money to help pay for the windmill. First, the students made and sold candle holders. Then, they used the money to buy the things they needed to build the windmill. They needed six metal barrels. They needed a car generator. And they needed four batteries.

The students cut the metal barrels in half. They put the barrels on a tall tower. The wind pushed the barrels around and around. The wind's power moved the generator. It made electricity. The electricity charged the batteries. And the batteries turned on the lights in the school.

"The students learned a lot about science," said their teacher. "And they learned how to use tools and how to work together on a job."

PLACES TO GO

A Visit to the Museum of Science and Industry

Go down into a coal mine. Watch baby chicks hatching. Walk through a large model of a human heart. You can do all these things at the Museum of Science and Industry. The museum is in Chicago, Illinois.

Millions of people visit the museum each year. They spend hours walking through the large showplace of exhibits. There is so much to see and do.

The museum has everything from old airplanes to solar-powered machines. In one exhibit, visitors ride through a coal mine. Visitors learn how special machines are used to mine coal. In another exhibit, visitors walk through a giant 5-meter-high model of the human heart. They learn how the heart works and how to take care of it. You will find visitors watching baby chicks hatch and discovering how the sun's rays are used for energy.

The museum helps people understand more about science. They see how science is used in transportation, space travel, farming, medicine, and health care.

PUZZLES TO DO

An Energy Source

Natural gas is used as energy to heat many houses and apartments. Find the way from the natural gas flame to the house.

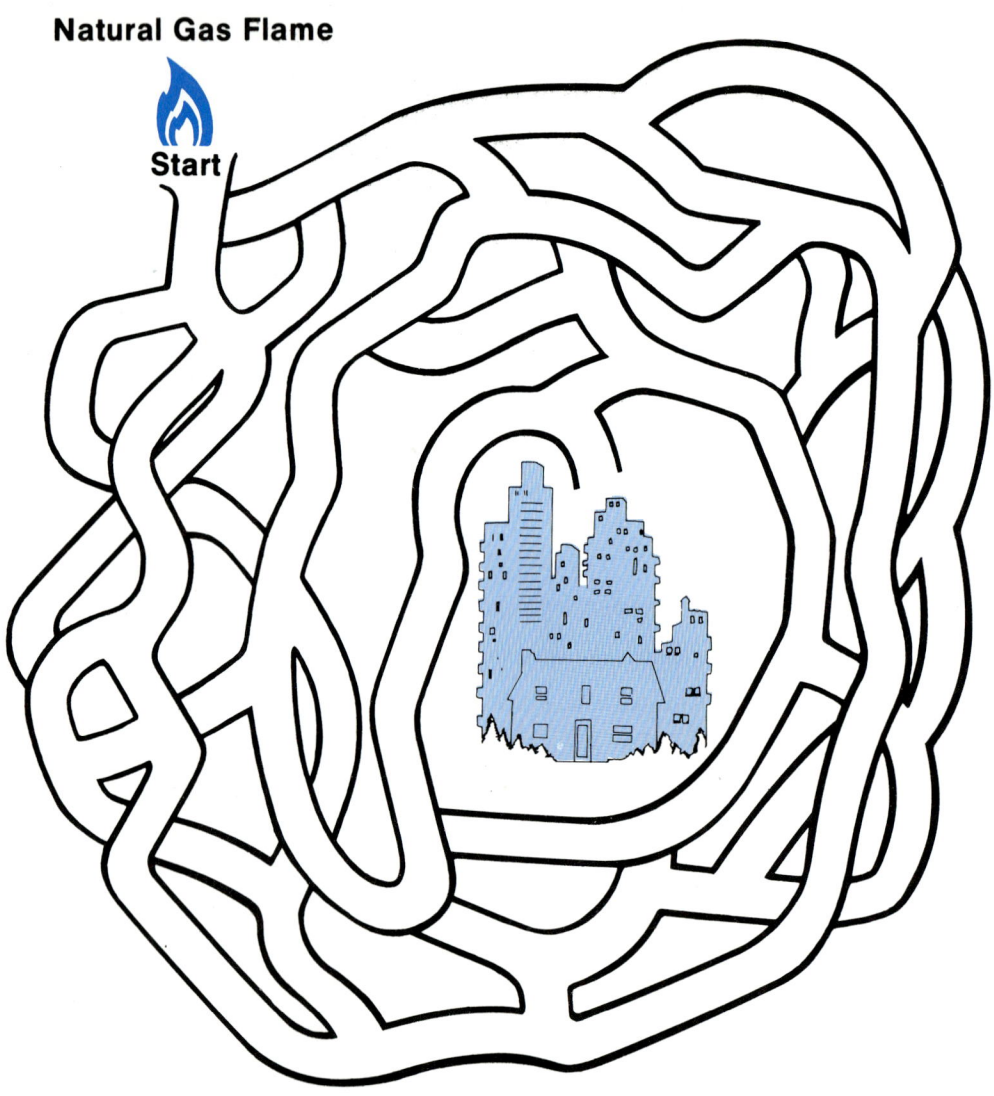

Products from Oil

Fill in the spaces with the names of 12 products that are made from oil. The names are listed below.

4-Letter Words

inks
rugs

5-Letter Words

tires
shoes

6-Letter Word

slacks

7-Letter Words

crayons
sponges
aspirin

8-Letter Words

snorkels
sneakers

10-Letter Words

telephones
parachutes

SCIENCE ADVENTURES

Investigating Paper Airplanes

Make a paper airplane like the model on page 95.
How far can you fly it? How long does your plane stay up?
Can you make a better plane than this one?

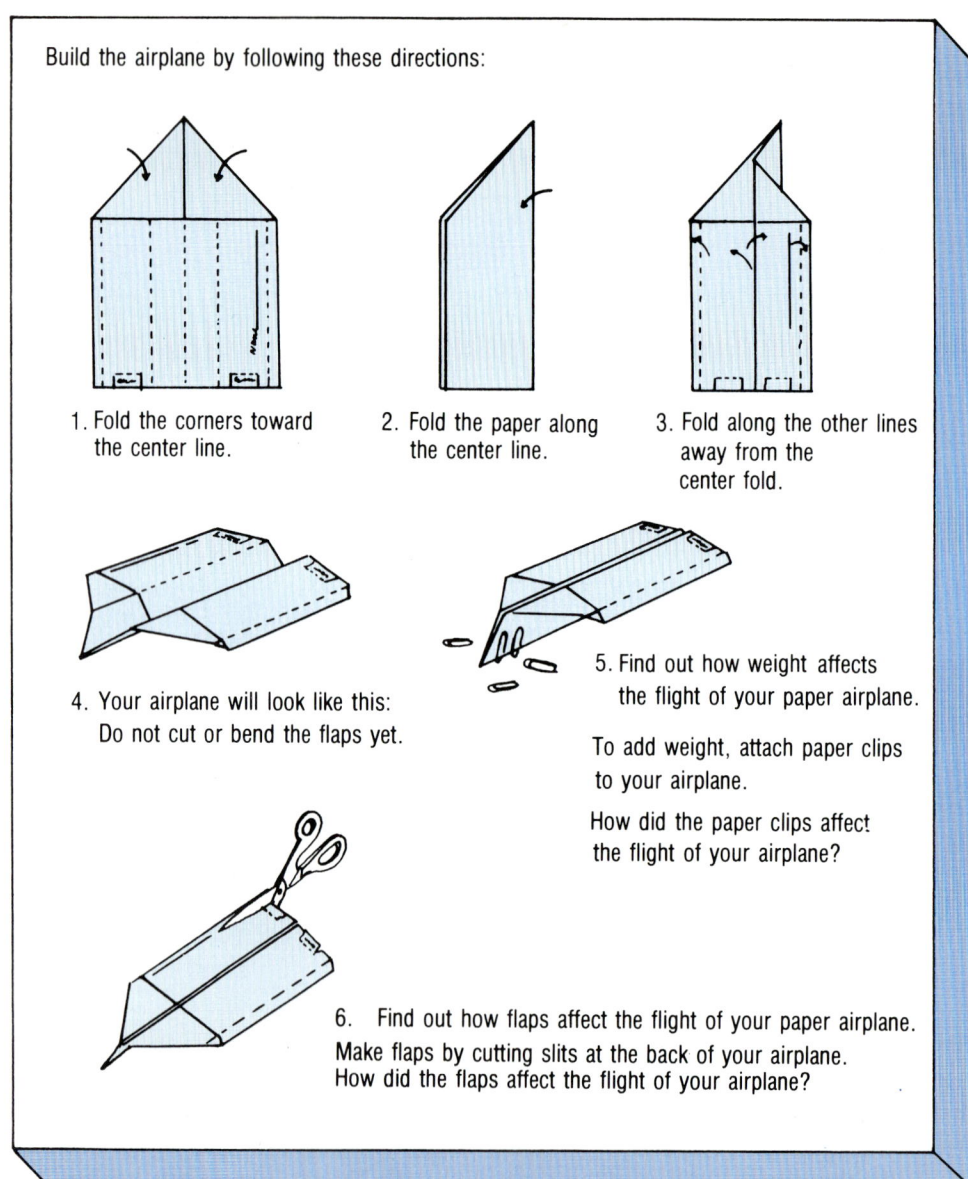

Build the airplane by following these directions:

1. Fold the corners toward the center line.

2. Fold the paper along the center line.

3. Fold along the other lines away from the center fold.

4. Your airplane will look like this: Do not cut or bend the flaps yet.

5. Find out how weight affects the flight of your paper airplane.

   To add weight, attach paper clips to your airplane.

   How did the paper clips affect the flight of your airplane?

6. Find out how flaps affect the flight of your paper airplane. Make flaps by cutting slits at the back of your airplane. How did the flaps affect the flight of your airplane?

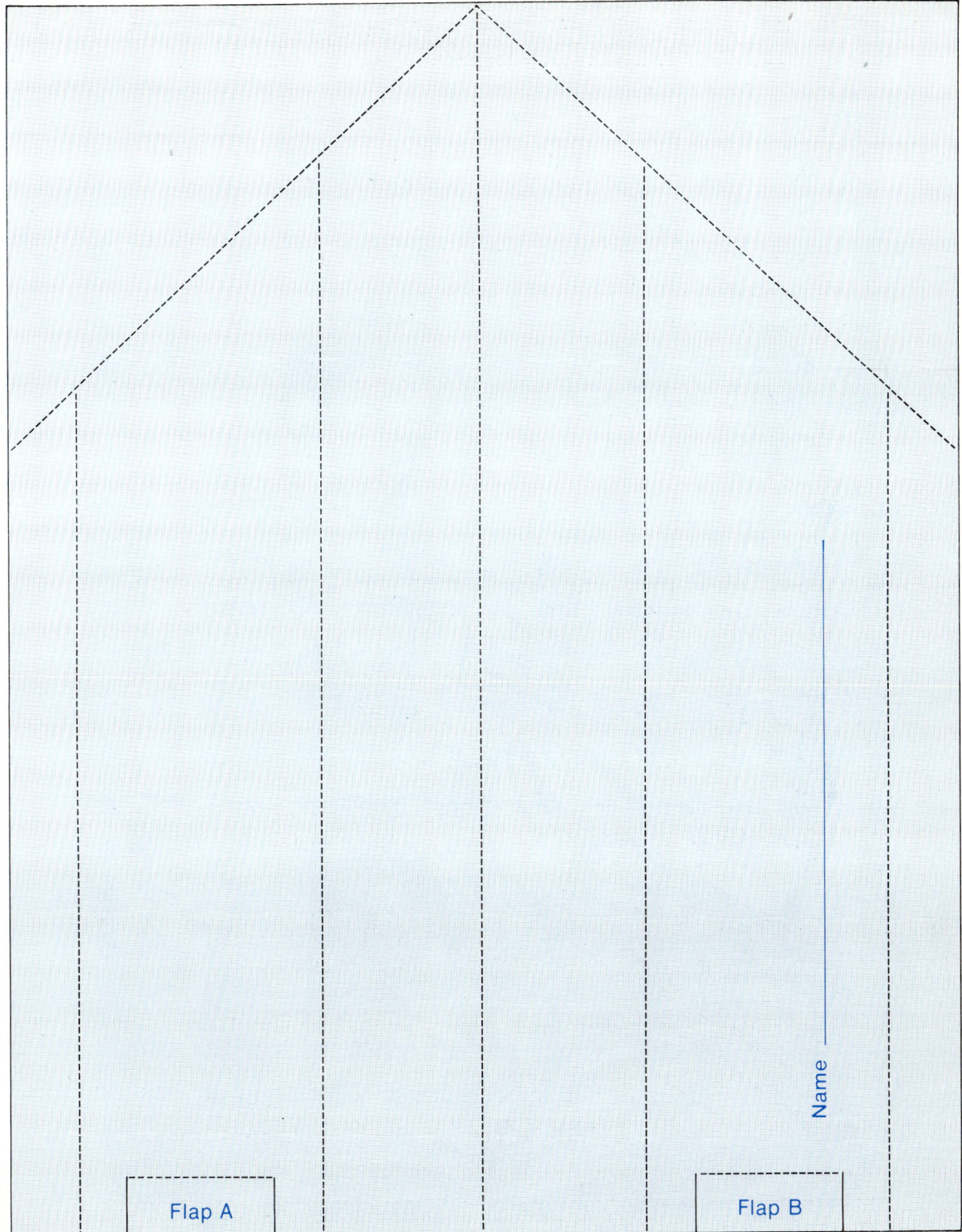

CAREERS IN SCIENCE

Dinosaurs lived a long time ago. We know about them because scientists found bones and fossils. A lot of people helped put this dinosaur back together. So we can learn about the kinds of animals that lived before us, and what happened to them.

Some of the people who helped to put this dinosaur together for a museum are: **paleontologists,** whose job is to study and learn about life as it was a long time ago;

geologists, who know about rocks and where dinosaur bones and fossils may be found;

artists, who work with paleontologists to put the bones together. Artists also draw pictures of what the creature would have looked like; and

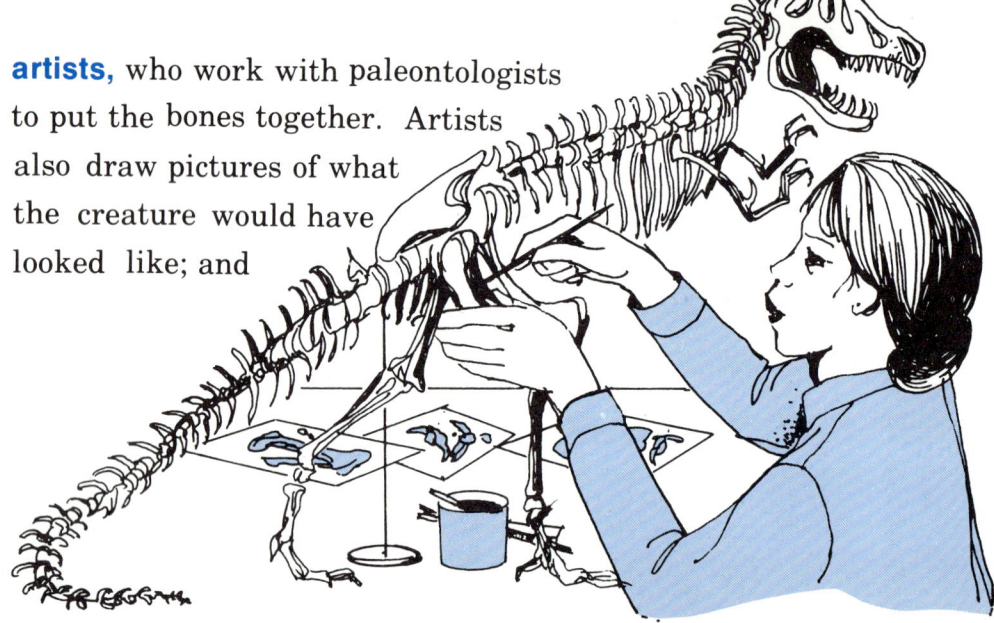

museum workers, who put the dinosaur where lots of people come to see it.

Can you think of other people who helped? Talk about it with a friend.

There are many careers in science that help bring good food to us.

Do you know the names of these careers?

Use the words below if you need help.

A person who grows food is called a _____.

A person who works with chemicals is called a _____.

A person who keeps animals healthy is called a _____.

A person who finds better ways to grow better plants is called a _____.

And a person who makes sure that our food is safe and good is called a _____.

Word List
FARMER
BOTANIST
VETERINARIAN
CHEMIST
FOOD INSPECTOR

Look at the career pictures. Now look at the puzzle.
Can you find all five science careers?

```
F O O D I N S P E C T O R
L A P Z O N K I N H I W A
T R U A K L R E B E R I H
H S H T S I F A R M E R A
V E T E R I N A R I A N T
X M Q B O T A N I S T Z P
A P I R A M I G H T E R M
```

Circle all the careers that you can find in the puzzle. Can you think of other science careers that help bring good food to us?

And now, make a hidden word puzzle with other science careers that you know about. Then, ask a friend to solve it.

Health Careers Are Important

There are many different kinds of careers in the health-service field. Look at the hospital. How many different health careers can you find? Look at the box at the bottom of the page for the names of these careers.

1. _____

2. _____

3. _____

4. _____

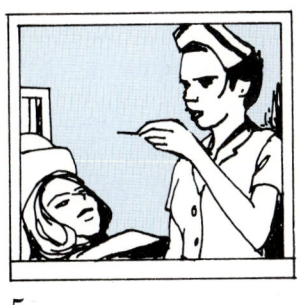
5. _____

6. _____

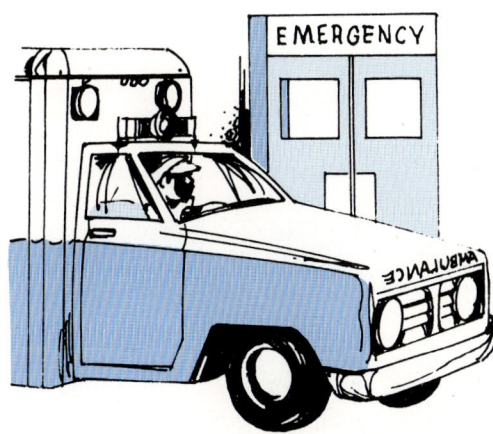
7. _____

Health work is important. Many people work together.
Can you identify these health careers?

pharmacist
medical records clerk
hospital orderly   nurse
X-ray technician
doctor   ambulance driver

101

WORDS TO KNOW

The following words are found in the stories throughout this book. The words are listed according to the page on which they appear.

Many of the science books and magazines that you use contain some or all of these words. So it is important that you know the meaning of each word as it is used in science. This will make it easier for you to read and understand science materials.

Use a dictionary or a glossary of science terms to find the meanings and pronunciations of those words that are not familiar to you. You may want to record this information in your own personal "word bank."

LIFE SCIENCE UNIT

p. 14
cave
centimeters
deer
forked
island
known
Komodo
largest
lizards
monitor lizard
photographs
skins
sticks
tongue
weigh

p.16
algae
carefully
happily
invisible
mostly
northern
polar
pool
scientists

p. 18
aside
chemical
DDT
endangered
fewer
hatch
insects
law
meters
reason
safely
watchers

p. 20
breathes
curls
gills
itself
lungs
necessary
reason
shallow
unlike

p. 22
alligator
bodies
camouflage
cannot
cheetahs
draw
floating
grasshoppers
insects
log
markings
moth
pink
polar
stems
stripes
zebras

p. 24
gorilla
language
mittens
vocabulary

p. 26
ant
bush
chew
fungi
leaf
leaves
sunlight

p. 28
beneath
floated
plates
safely
scientists
spiders
submarines
travel
undersea

p. 30
body
nutrients

p. 32
cavity
check
cheese
crooked
dental
dentist
difficult
firm
floss
gums
healthy
loss

material
pink
remind

p. 34
areas
arrived
bamboo
disagree
kilograms
member
meters
pandas
scientists
slowly
types
weigh
workers

p. 36
body
bunny
extra
hairy
rat
roots
spines
stems
sunlight
type
usually

p. 38
flavor
pods
raw
scientists
succeeded
sweetest
tastier
tested
tough
usually
vine
wonderful

p. 40
cannot
dinosaur
everywhere
fan
fossils
ginkgoes
grown
soot
waxy

EARTH-SPACE SCIENCE UNIT

p. 50
bones
centimeters
claws
deadly
dinosaurs
easily
kilograms
larger
probably
protection
quickly
reason
scientists
sharp
terrible
weighed

p. 52
bones
bubbling
builders
extinct
gas
oil
pits
pools
saber-toothed
shiny
someone
sticky
stuck
tar
thousands
workers

p. 54
astronauts
billion
formed
landings
life
likely
moon
samples
scientists
space
studying
travel

p. 56
longer
nearly
scientists
seasons
storm
twice

p. 58
hunters
hurricanes
information
instruments
kilometers
plane
scientists
storms
warnings

p. 60
areas
arid
body
contain
floating
icebergs
kilometers
located
meters
mostly
slowly
tow
tug

p. 62
cannot
glacier
hidden
iceberg
planes
rising
steer
suddenly
thunder
torn
usually

p. 64
aboard
cameras
completely
diving
freezing
headlights
hook
kilometers
later
level
minerals
pilot
samples
scientists
scoops
study
submersible
temperature
travel
windows

PHYSICAL SCIENCE UNIT

p. 74
control
float
kites
pilot
rising
soar
steer
thermal

p. 76
balloonists
breathtaking
discovery
finally
float
gas burner
hooked
nylon
straw
travel

p. 78
cannot
cost
easily
energy
free
longer
modern
oil
powered
sailboats
sailors

p. 80
bands
breathe
dangerous
loss
measured
planes
tests
unwanted

p. 82
battery
carbon
cells
chemical
connected
electric
electricity
flashlights
flows
material
paste
tape recorders
rod
zinc

p. 84
cannot
cloud
collect
collector
flows
heat
hidden
panels
pipes
reason
solar
sunshine

p. 86
advantages
bigger
dirty
easily
energy
explode
fuel
gas
gasoline
however
hydrogen
powers
safer
space
spaceships
substance
tanks

p. 88
electrical power
film
form
fuel
future
heat
movie
material
oil
petroleum
planes
plastics
power
safety
scientists
shampoo

PROGRESS CHART FOR LIFE SCIENCE UNIT

Questions Page	Comprehension Question Numbers				Total Number Correct per Story
	Science Vocabulary	Literal	Interpretive	Applied	
15	1	2	3,4,5		
17	1	2	3,4,5		
19	1	2,3	4,5		
21		1,2,3	4,5		
23	1	2,3	4,5		
25	1	2	3,4,5		
27	1	2,3	4,5		
29	1	2,3	4	5	
31	1	2	3	4,5	
33	1	2,3	4,5		
35	1	2,3	4,5		
37	1	2,3,4	5		
39	1	2,3	4,5		
41	1	2	3,4	5	
TOTAL Correct by Question Type					

KEEPING A RECORD OF YOUR PROGRESS

The Progress Charts on these pages are for use with the questions that follow the stories in the Life Science, Earth-Space Science, and Physical Science Units. Keeping a record of your progress will help you to see how well you are doing and where you need to improve. Use the charts in the following way:

After you have checked your answers, look at the first column, headed "Questions Page." Read down the column until you find the row with the page number of the questions you have completed. Put an X through the number of each question in the row that you answered correctly. Add the number of correct answers, and write your total score in the last column in that row.

After you have done the questions for several stories, check to see which questions you answered correctly. Which ones were incorrect? Is there a pattern? For example, you may find that you have answered most of the literal comprehension questions correctly but that you are having difficulty answering the applied comprehension questions. If so, then this is an area in which you need help.

When you have completed all the stories in a unit, write the total number of correct answers at the bottom of each column.

PROGRESS CHART FOR PHYSICAL SCIENCE UNIT

Questions Page	Comprehension Question Numbers					Total Number Correct per Story
	Science Vocabulary	Literal	Interpretive	Applied	
75	1	2,3	4,5		
77	1	2,3	4,5		
79	1	2,3	4,5		
81		1,2,3	4,5		
83	1	2,3,4	5		
85	1	2,3	4,5		
87	1	2,3	4,5		
89	1	2,3	4,5		

TOTAL Correct by Question Type

PROGRESS CHART FOR EARTH-SPACE SCIENCE UNIT

Questions Page	Comprehension Question Numbers					Total Number Correct per Story
	Science Vocabulary	Literal	Interpretive	Applied	
51	1	2	3,4,5		
53	1	2	3,4,5		
55	1	2	3,4,5		
57		1,2,3	4,5		
59	1	2,3	4,5		
61	1	2,3	4,5		
63	1	2	3,4,5		
65	1	2,3	4,5		

TOTAL Correct by Question Type

BIBLIOGRAPHY

Books on Life Science

Anderson, Lucia. *The Smallest Life Around Us,*
 illustrated by Leigh Grant. New York: Crown Publishers, 1978.

Ballestrino, Philip. *The Skeleton Inside You.* New York: Thomas Y. Crowell, 1971.

Behnke, Frances. *What We Find When We Look Under Rocks.* New York: McGraw-Hill, 1971.

Berger, Melvin. *Jobs That Save Our Environment: Exploring Careers.*
 New York: Lothrop, 1973.

Bradenberg, Aliki. *Green Grass and White Milk.* New York: Thomas Y. Crowell, 1974.

Buxton, Ralph. *Nature's Gliders: The Flying Squirrels,*
 illustrated by Angus M. Babcock. Chicago: Childrens Press, 1975.

Cole, Joanna. *Plants in Winter.* New York: Thomas Y. Crowell, 1974.

Cooke, Ann. *Giraffes at Home.* New York: Thomas Y. Crowell, 1974.

Franklin, Watts. *Oranges, Peanuts, Tomatoes.* Chicago: Childrens Press, 1978.

Freedman, Russell. *Hanging On.* New York: Holiday, 1977.

Gordon, Bernard L. and Ester S. Gordon. *There Really Was a Dodo.*
 New York: Henry Z. Walck, Inc., 1974.

Halmi, Robert. *Zoos of the World.* New York: Four Winds Press, 1975.

Hussong, Clara. *Birds.* Racine, Wisconsin: Golden Press, 1973.

Jacobs, Francine. *A Secret Language of Animals: Communication by Pheromones.*
 New York: Morrow Junior Books, 1976.

McCoy, J. J. *A Sea of Troubles.* New York: Seabury Press, 1975.

McNamara, Louise and Ada Litchfield. *Your Busy Brain.*
 Boston: Little, Brown & Co., 1973.

Millard, Adele. *Plants for Kids to Grow Indoors.* New York: Sterling, 1975.

Parker, Alice. *Terrariums.* New York: Franklin Watts, 1977.

Pemns, Christopher. *Birds: Their Life, Their Ways, Their World.*
 New York: Harry N. Abrams, Inc., 1976.

Pringle, Lawrence. *Twist, Wiggle, and Squirm: A Book About Earthworms.*
 New York: Thomas Y. Crowell, 1973.

Rahn, Joan Elma. *Nature in the City: Plants,*
 illustrated by Stef Leinwohl and Paul Westermann. Chicago: Childrens Press, 1977.

Rau, Margaret. *Musk Oxen: Bearded Ones of the Arctic.*
 New York: Thomas Y. Crowell, 1976.

Ross, Wilda. *The Rain Forest: What Lives There.*
 New York: Coward, McCann & Geoghegan, 1977.

Selsam, Millicent E. and Joyce Hunt. *How Animals Sleep.*
 New York: Scholastic Book Services, 1962.

———. *Land of the Giant Tortoise: The Story of the Galapagos.*
New York: Four Winds Press, 1977.

Showers, Paul. *What Happens to a Hamburger.* New York: Thomas Y. Crowell, 1970.

Silverstein, Dr. Alvin and Virginia B. Silverstein.
Itch, Sniffle & Sneeze: All About Asthma, Hay Fever, and Other Allergies.
New York: Four Winds Press, 1978.

Simon, Seymour. *About Your Heart.* New York: McGraw-Hill, 1974.

Thompson-Cloudsley, John. *The Desert.* East Rutherford, New Jersey: G.P. Putnam's Sons, 1977.

Walsh, Ame Batterbervey. *A Gardening Book: Indoors & Outdoors.* New York: Atheneum, 1976.

Waters, John F. *Camels: Ships of the Desert.* New York: Thomas Y. Crowell, 1976.

Wohlrabe, Raymond A. *Exploring the World of Leaves.* New York: Thomas Y. Crowell, 1976.

Zim, Herbert, *Owls.* New York: Morrow, 1977.

Books on Earth-Space Science

Anderson, Madelyn Klein. *Iceberg Alley.* New York: Julian Messner, 1976.

Brandenberg, Aliki. *Fossils Tell of Long Ago.* New York: Thomas Y. Crowell, 1972.

Branley, Franklyn M. *Floating and Sinking.* New York: Thomas Y. Crowell, 1967.

———. *Sunshine Makes the Seasons.* New York: Thomas Y. Crowell, 1974.

Brindze, Ruth. *Hurricanes—Monster Storms from the Sea.* New York: Atheneum, 1973.

Brown, Joseph E. *The Sea's Harvest.* New York: Dodd, Mead, 1975.

——— and Ann E. Brown. *Harness the Wind.* New York: Dodd, Mead, 1977.

Dwiggins, Don. *Riders of the Wind—The Story of Ballooning.*
New York: Hawthorn Books, 1973.

Fodor, R.V. *Meteorites: Stones from the Sky.* New York: Dodd, Mead, 1976.

Gans, Roma. *Icebergs.* New York: Thomas Y. Crowell, 1964.

Goldreich, Gloria and Esther Goldreich. *What Can She Be? A Geologist.*
New York: Lothrop, Lee & Shepard, 1976.

Klaits, Barrie. *When You Find a Rock: A Field Guide.*
New York: Macmillan, 1976.

Kohn, Bernice, *Communications Satellites: Message Centers in Space.*
New York: Four Winds Press, 1975.

Milgram, Harry. *Understanding Weather,* revised edition. New York: Crowell, Collin, 1970.

Pringle, Lawrence. *The Hidden World: Life Under a Rock.* New York: Macmillan, 1977.

Rey, H.A. *Find the Constellations.* Boston: Houghton Mifflin, 1976.

Ryan, Martha. *Weather.* New York: Franklin Watts, 1976.

Schlein, Miriam. *On the Track of the Mystery Animal.*
New York: Four Winds Press, 1978.

Smith, Norman F. *Space: What's Out There?*
New York: Coward, McCann & Geoghegan, 1976.

Tangborn, Wendell V. *Glaciers*. New York: Thomas Y. Crowell, 1965.

Wyler, Rose and Gerald Ames. *Secrets in Stones*. New York: Four Winds Press, 1972.

Books on Physical Science

Amery, Heather and Angela Littler. *The Know How Book of Experiments with Batteries and Magnets*. New York: Sterling, 1976.

Bendick, Jeanne. *Heat and Temperature*. New York: Franklin Watts, 1974.

Berger, Melvin. *Energy from the Sun*. New York: Thomas Y. Crowell, 1976.

Branley, Franklyn M. *Gravity Is a Mystery*. New York: Thomas Y. Crowell, 1970.

Doty, Roy, with Len Maar. *Where Are You Going with That Energy?* New York: Doubleday, 1977.

Epstein, Sam and Beryl Epstein. *The First Book of Electricity*. New York: Franklin Watts. 1977.

Goldin, Augusta. *Salt*. New York: Thomas Y. Crowell, 1966.

Keifer, Irene. *Underground Furnaces: The Story of Geothermal Energy*. New York: Morrow, 1976.

Knight, David C. *Harnessing the Sun: The Story of Solar Energy*. New York: Morrow Junior Books, 1976.

Ridiman, Bob. *Simple Science Fun*. New York: Parents' Magazine Press, 1972.

Schneider, Herman and Nina Schneider. *Science Fun with a Flashlight*. New York: McGraw-Hill, 1975.

Wyler, Rose. *What Happens If: Science Experiments You Can Do by Yourself*. New York: Walker & Co. 1974.

METRIC TABLE

This table tells you how to change customary units of measure to metric units of measure. The answers you get will not be exact.

LENGTH

Symbol	When You Know	Multiply by	To Find	Symbol
in	inches	2.5	centimeters	cm
ft	feet	30	centimeters	cm
yd	yards	0.9	meters	m
mi	miles	1.6	kilometers	km

AREA

Symbol	When You Know	Multiply by	To Find	Symbol
in^2	square inches	6.5	square centimeters	cm^2
ft^2	square feet	0.09	square meters	m^2
yd^2	square yards	0.8	square meters	m^2
mi^2	square miles	2.6	square kilometers	km^2
	acres	0.4	hectares	ha

MASS (weight)

Symbol	When You Know	Multiply by	To Find	Symbol
oz	ounces	28	grams	g
lb	pounds	0.45	kilograms	kg
	short tons (2000 lb)	0.9	tonnes	t

VOLUME

Symbol	When You Know	Multiply by	To Find	Symbol
tsp	teaspoons	5	milliliters	mL
Tbsp	tablespoons	15	milliliters	mL
fl oz	fluid ounces	30	milliliters	mL
c	cups	0.24	liters	L
pt	pints	0.47	liters	L
qt	quarts	0.95	liters	L
gal	gallons	3.8	liters	L
ft^3	cubic feet	0.03	cubic meters	m^3
yd^3	cubic yards	0.76	cubic meters	m^3

TEMPERATURE (exact)

Symbol	When You Know	Multiply by	To Find	Symbol
°F	Fahrenheit temperature	5/9 (after subtracting 32)	Celsius temperature	°C

METRIC TABLE

This table tells you how to change metric units of measure to customary units of measure. The answers you get will not be exact.

LENGTH

Symbol	When You Know	Multiply by	To Find	Symbol
mm	millimeters	0.04	inches	in
cm	centimeters	0.4	inches	in
m	meters	3.3	feet	ft
m	meters	1.1	yards	yd
km	kilometers	0.6	miles	mi

AREA

Symbol	When You Know	Multiply by	To Find	Symbol
cm^2	square centimeters	0.16	square inches	in^2
m^2	square meters	1.2	square yards	yd^2
km^2	square kilometers	0.4	square miles	mi^2
ha	hectares (10,000 m^2)	2.5	acres	

MASS (weight)

Symbol	When You Know	Multiply by	To Find	Symbol
g	grams	0.035	ounces	oz
kg	kilograms	2.2	pounds	lb
t	tonnes (1000 kg)	1.1	short tons	

VOLUME

Symbol	When You Know	Multiply by	To Find	Symbol
mL	milliliters	0.03	fluid ounces	fl oz
L	liters	2.1	pints	pt
L	liters	1.06	quarts	qt
L	liters	0.26	gallons	gal
m^3	cubic meters	35	cubic feet	ft^3
m^3	cubic meters	1.3	cubic yards	yd^3

TEMPERATURE (exact)

Symbol	When You Know	Multiply by	To Find	Symbol
°C	Celsius temperature	9/5 (then add 32)	Fahrenheit temperature	°F